PIECE BY PIECE

PIECE BY PIECE

HOW I BUILT MY LIFE
(NO INSTRUCTIONS REQUIRED)

DAVID AGUILAR and FERRAN AGUILAR

TRANSLATED BY LAWRENCE SCHIMEL

amazon**crossing kids**

PIECE BY PIECE

I've often been asked what it feels like when you're missing half an arm. And the truth is, even now at twenty years old, I still don't know. What do you feel if you are missing a finger? Count them for me, OK? Stop reading and count the fingers you have.

One,

two,

three,

four,

five,

six,

seven,

eight,

nine,

ten!

What do you feel when you're missing the eleventh finger?

Whoa! You don't know what that feels like, right?

I count to five. You count to ten. I am not missing anything. Neither are you.

And if you are part of that small group of us who don't reach ten, like me, then you're not missing anything, either. Really. At first you don't see it, because your entire life you've heard the word *without* or been told you're "missing" something. Well, I'm here to tell you: you're not missing anything; in fact, you have a surplus.

A surplus of possibilities.

Having said that, I think we can begin. Does that sound good?

It all began . . .

ROSES, CARNATIONS, ETC.

It all began in a hospital in Andorra, in room 102.

My grandparents, my great-grandmother, and my aunts were all waiting—waiting for me.

They already knew me: I was David, the strong and healthy child my parents were expecting, whom my grandparents already adored, and the whole family was impatient for me to be born.

My grandmother Basilisa, who I usually just called Abu (short for *abuela* or grandmother) or Abu Basi, sat there nervously rubbing her fingers, feeling emotional as she constantly twisted her wedding ring. She was waiting for her son, my father, to open the door at any moment with a smile on his lips and me in his arms, wrapped in the swaddling blanket she herself had sewn with such care, and . . .

And yes, I suppose that's more or less what happened.

Meanwhile, my father paced the long hallways from the surgery to the waiting room, eyes full of tears, overwhelmed by the circumstances. He didn't dare enter the room right away. Finally he opened the door—and there I was in his arms, wrapped in the swaddling clothes. But my father was missing a smile, and I was missing an arm, and the swaddling absorbed the tears that fell from his eyes. Things that happened.

"Why that sad face, Ferran?" my *abuela* asked, getting up. "Is everything OK? Is Nathalie OK?"

But my father couldn't manage to speak a word, and the others couldn't stop staring at him in fear. Everyone had paled when they saw him come in, whiter than the coat of any doctor in that hospital. And there I was, unaware of everything, of the fear my family felt, of my *abuela*'s unease and my father's grief. So unaware that, well, I don't even remember any of that, of course; I know it because I've been told the story so many times.

"So David . . . so . . . ," he tried to answer.

"David what?" At that moment, my *abu* came closer and uncovered part of the swaddling and saw for the first time my *muñón*, the stump where my right arm ended. "Oh, Ferran . . ." That was all she could say.

"Just that . . . Just that . . . Otherwise the doctor says he's perfect."

Basi began to caress my cheeks, my brow, my little head. She grabbed my little hand, the one I do have, and rubbed it with her thumb. Then she kissed my forehead before saying, "Well, of course he's perfect. Can't you see?"

Curiously, that kiss I do remember.

You can imagine how the rest of that day went. And that week, and practically half my life. Looks of pity, like old friends, have always accompanied me. I even call them by their names, and we greet one another: there's the *penasco* (from *pena* and *asco* in Spanish, when people feel pity but also disgust, as if my stump were going to bite them!), the *penalivio* (from *pena* and *alivio*, when they feel sorry for your parents but relief their own child was born with two arms), and the *penobre* (*pena* and *pobre* merged into a simple "oh, poor thing"). But I'll tell you all about this later, because there's enough material for an entire chapter or even a few of them. The thing is, my mother woke up from the anesthesia a little while later, frightened at not seeing me, and when she could, she wept, of course, because it was a surprise for everyone.

As if wanting to console us—almost without our realizing it and despite it being February 25—spring arrived early: the room filled with flowers, and the flowers hid words like "I'm so sorry," "Have strength," and "Our unconditional support" in the form of cards that pricked more than any thorns might. As soon as they heard the news, distant relatives, neighbors, and acquaintances all responded in this way, so that pollen flooded the room and made a permanent cloud that floated above the bouquets, which wound up piled outside, beside the door.

Right now, the truth is I wish I could go back in time and appear there, in front of room 102, to sidestep the roses, push through the daisies, open the door, and tell my parents, "Don't worry, you've done a good job."

At that moment, my missing arm seemed to them the greatest surprise of their lives. But the true surprises would come later, with what they and I would achieve. They'd wind up surprising themselves, and I'd wind up surprising the world. Mamá and Papá are now so proud of their work as parents.

Calling what's different a *dis*ability doesn't do more than give anyone who is different nothing to live for. But I learned this only by traveling down the difficult path.

DISABLED?

A list of things my father thought he wouldn't be able to do with me:

- Play video games together
- Play guitar
- Take me skiing
- Show me how to ride a bike
- Go bike riding on Sundays after showing me how to ride a bike

A list of things I've done with my father:

- Play video games together
- Play a drum pad and compose
- Go skiing

- Learn to ride a bike
- Go bike riding on Sundays after learning how to ride a bike
- Ride an electric scooter and represent a major brand
- Do aeromodelling
- Go kayaking
- Swim
- Go climbing

Mamá and I spent a few weeks in the hospital. She was there because of complications from the cesarean; I was there, of course, because of my *bracito*, my little arm. That's what everyone called it: *bracito*. In addition to words like *without* and *missing*, I've also had to get used to suffixes for diminutives, even long after I stopped being little myself. I accepted it, because that's how I saw myself on many occasions: diminished, minuscule . . . in short, *-ito*. It wasn't until later, after always demonstrating I wasn't, that I decided to stop feeling that way.

The doctors observed me, did tests, and decided it would be best for me to remain in the hospital with my mother. They didn't make any diagnosis that was especially clear: a regular malformation, a nonformation . . . Whatever it was, there were no signs of anything malignant. The *bracito* was missing, and that was it. So while they verified their tests, I stayed there with my mother, and with my father, who wouldn't leave us.

Nor would my *abuela*; she was always there. Every day. She brought food for Papá, who made full use of the scant paternity leave granted back then, and she spent hours with me in her arms.

"I don't know what we're going to do, Mamá," my father told her. Doubts ate away at him; he just couldn't stop wondering if it would be difficult.

"With what?" she answered.

"With the child!" he answered, as if it wasn't obvious. Abu Basi slowly wandered from one side of the room to the other, cradling me so I stayed asleep, and she asked him to lower his voice so he didn't wake my mother. "What will the children at school say to him? How will he tie his shoes? How will he ride a bike? Or drive a car?"

Calm as only she can be in the face of this kind of situation (and always the voice of reason and love), she sat down next to my father and, with me still cradled in her hands, kissed my cheeks and tickled my nose. My father remembers it with absolute clarity, and that's how he recounted it one Christmas when I opened—with more dexterity than my sister—the gift that contained my first LEGO (a Speed Racer car, which was really cool, by the way). And what she told him then was burned into his memory as if by fire: "Ferran, it's very simple. What we need to do with this boy is love him and take care of him. Kids at school, let them say what they like. To heck with them. As for his shoes, I'll be there to tie them for him whenever he needs. As far as the bicycle goes, we'll find a solution. And as for driving, aren't there automatic cars these days? In any case, I'm sure he'll wind up being so clever he'll have enough money to hire a chauffeur!"

My father fell silent. In that moment of pain it was really hard for him to see beyond my arm. It was much harder for him than for my mother, there's no doubt.

Every time he recounts this anecdote, he does so with the same expression of astonishment. Every Christmas, every birthday, in front of the cake—the candles that keep growing in number with each year, lit up with the scent of burning wax—my father narrates this episode with the same mix of tenderness and disbelief.

ROMPECUELLOS

A day came when I left the hospital in my mother's arms, with my father beside us, asking incessantly if we needed anything. My grandparents followed us to the car, telling my father to stop bothering us, to not worry so much; everything was fine.

Discharged at last! Yes, it would all turn out just fine. I was perfect. I was healthy. I just had a little defect, an *-ito* that we could all put into perspective over time thanks to Peggy Cerqueda and her mother, Dr. Doncel, who you'll meet later. It seemed the flowers had disappeared from the door of the room; the funeral for my arm had been suspended, and everyone, even the protagonists, went home with the promise to forget about it. Hope had settled in our hearts like a welcomed guest. Even still, not all the flowers wilted during those two weeks; some survived, remaining lovely and lush, firm in stem and with buds that had yet to open and flourish. The nurses bundled them into a bouquet they prepared for us as a farewell gift, and although neither my parents nor my grandparents wished to see any more flowers for a long time, they accepted the bouquet and carefully stowed it in the trunk of the car.

The path back, my first journey home, was strange and emotional. My mother has told me a few times that she was so tired it was hard for her to taste the joy, and my father didn't stop drying his eyes, which filled with tears of happiness at being able to return home with his son. Everything seemed unreal, although the world was exactly as it had been before: the blue sky seemed green, and the sun emitted cold instead of heat. Nonetheless, we felt good. Our happiness was overwhelming happiness but discreet and fragile, for it had suffered too many blows and perhaps wouldn't be able to withstand any more. We had no idea then how many more we would receive, how many more it would take to make us strong enough.

When we arrived home, the first thing my father did was lead us to the bedroom so we could rest. Since I was asleep, my mother settled me in the crib. Meanwhile, my grandparents helped unload the trunk, and without asking anyone, Abu Basi cunningly placed that lovely bouquet in the middle of the dining room, resignedly admiring its beauty. My father returned to the garage and finished taking everything out of the car. Then he looked in the mailbox to see if there were any letters. As soon as he opened it, he regretted having done so—but who could ever imagine that something so ordinary as opening the mailbox would cause him such torment? He expected to find bank statements, electricity bills. Instead he found a promotional pamphlet for an orthopedist.

That was the first moment he realized that, no matter how much we accepted the situation, people would always point at me. I would always be special, strange, different. My arm—my lack of an arm—was like a terrible mark that would accompany me my entire life.

And like that moment, there came others.

One of the things I remember most vividly from my childhood is going out on the street. Stepping on the sidewalk, going for a walk, or playing in the park was like falling into another dimension or, even worse: entering the real world, where people made it very clear I was not normal.

Now when I think back it seems surreal to me. Yes, people, I am missing half an arm! Put down your phones; there's no need to call the investigators from *Cuarto Milenio* or those kids from *Stranger Things*. But when I was four or five years old, I couldn't think that way. So in those moments I'd always place myself between Mamá and Papá. I hid my missing arm—and my guilt for not having it—from the gazes of passersby, because that's how they made me feel: guilty, as if I'd done something wrong and they were going to yell at me any moment now. And it wasn't enough to just look at me; after they passed, they'd turn around to check: yes, he's *manco*, the poor boy. He's got only one hand.

"Hey, David," my father said one day.

"Mmm?" I answered, already in a bad mood because a woman was staring at me with a look of horror on her face.

"Do you think she is going to turn around?"

"Who?"

To my surprise, he indicated with his head the woman who wouldn't take her eyes off my *bracito*.

I looked at him questioningly.

"Go on, say it. Do you think she'll turn around?"

"Yes!" I didn't need to think twice.

"What are you two whispering about?" Mamá asked.

The woman passed us and . . .

"Now you'll see," I answered my father, and both of us turned at the same time to check. And she did turn to look at us, so fast she almost broke her neck. But when she saw us watching her, she turned red as a tomato and whipped her head around to face forward once more.

"Take that!" we said in unison, high-fiving each other.

From that day on, it turned into a game: *rompecuellos*, or breaking necks. And that's how Papá shredded my fear of going out onto the street, just like he'd shredded that pamphlet from the orthopedist.

LACES

One day, many years later, as I was leaving school, one of my classmates saw me fiddling with the car keys. "You drive?" he asked me, surprised.

"Um . . ." I was caught unaware, because what was so strange about my driving? "Yeah, of course, *tío*. I repeated a year. I'm eighteen already. I got my license over the break."

More than clarifying things, I seemed to confuse him even more. He wrinkled his brow so much I thought his forehead might cave in. Only then did I begin to realize what was going through his head.

It wasn't long before he verbalized it: "But . . . how do you drive?" His gaze indicated my missing arm.

I smiled. By then I already had an answer for everything. "With my hand, of course!" I said, raising my left arm.

"But how do you shift gears?"

I smiled even more.

"With my mouth!"

He was flabbergasted, and I got into the car. I turned on the ignition and pulled out, leaving him there with his mouth open. Did he really not know that automatic cars exist, without any need to shift gears? But no, I knew, as I had known my whole life, that what was really difficult to know—and especially to understand—is how someone who is not like you can do the same things you can.

I know this very well, believe me, because this was exactly my parents' challenge. And also mine. It was for a long time. I don't blame people or myself. Speaking clearly, what happens is that there is no one to blame: there is just ignorance, and prejudices, and loneliness. Dark nights, entire afternoons filled with worry. How would David get ahead? What would become of him?

"What we need to do with the boy is to love him and take care of him." Abuela Basi's words echoed every day at home, especially when my parents had to go back to work.

She took care of me during the day with all her love and experience. Her mother had been a midwife, and she had been a daughter with a lot of sensitivity who had learned a lot from her.

No one better than my *abuela* Basi could have been in charge of me during those first years. She cradled me

with one arm and read gossip magazines like *Pronto* with
the other. That's how she was: full of light, affection, and
good works. But her words and optimism weren't enough
for my parents. No matter that she might see the light at
the end of the tunnel; they saw only doubts and worries:
Would I always depend on them? What would become of
me when they weren't there? Would I live life less because
I needed to always be glued to their sides? Would I never
find independence or have a chance at a "normal" life? They
couldn't seem to emerge from their spiral of *dis-*, nor could
they see the magic of the eleventh finger. It's hard to climb
out of a well if you have only one arm, you know?

Luckily, all that changed thanks to two very special
people.

"Come in," my father said without getting up from the
desk in his office. He was staring at his computer screen,
busy checking account after account. Two of his cowork-
ers—Teo, who was the head of their branch, and Toni,
another colleague—knocked on the door, then opened it.

"Aren't you coming to eat, Ferran?"

"No, thanks. I've brought lunch from home today."

"It's been a long while since you've come with us to the
bar."

During that time, the first year after my birth, my
father had closed himself off. Despite the ray of light he'd

had in the hospital, he just couldn't stop worrying about what my future might be like. As a result, he was less sociable than usual. But that day something changed. Teo had always trusted my father and, with my birth, had become an unconditional pillar of support for him. He understood right away my father needed more time to be with me and my mother those first months. So when Teo and Toni insisted that they missed him, my father decided to go to lunch with them that day.

These colleagues from work were the ones to recommend that my dad call Dr. Doncel.

"It seems her daughter is just like your son."

"Like my son?"

"Like your son."

"You mean to say . . . she's missing an arm?"

"Yes, it seems her daughter is also missing an arm, like David. You should call her. Look, her number is . . ."

Papá thought about it for a long time and finally discussed it with my mother after she woke up from a long siesta.

"What do you say, Nathalie? Shall we call?"

"I don't know. It's very late. You should wait until tomorrow," she answered. But my father, despite her sleepy tone, recognized in her voice the same roller coaster of emotions he had felt when Teo and Toni gave him the number.

And what a roller coaster it was and always would be! We in the Aguilar Amphoux family have ridden it thousands of times. We know its every curve and all its highs and lows as if we'd designed it ourselves. We're like those die-hard fans who go from one amusement park to another to try every roller coaster in the country. It must be said that every time—*every single time*—we disembarked from it having learned something. Who wouldn't buy a ticket in that case?

"Why wait?" Papá said. "We have the solution in front of us, six digits away. Ring ring."

"Because it's late. And you don't know if that woman has the solution. Besides, you might wake the baby."

"I'll go in the hallway."

"You're not going to talk with that doctor without my hearing everything," she said.

"Then you leave me no other choice," he responded and punched in the phone number before my mother could protest.

After three long rings, during which my mother scrunched her face in disapproval, Dr. Doncel picked up.

"Hello?" they heard from the other end of the line.

"Good evening, Doctor. My name is Ferran Aguilar. I'm sorry to bother you at this time, but . . . you see . . . I have a son who's like your daughter."

The conversation didn't last long. Not only was it late, but also the doctor had already heard everything she needed: "We'd like to meet you," "We're afraid," "We don't know how to face this."

"Don't say anything else," she interrupted. "We'll meet tomorrow, if that's good for you?"

After exchanging a few more details, the call ended.

"And so?" my mother asked.

Papá only smiled and approached my crib.

"Tomorrow we'll find out," he replied. "For good or bad, we'll know something."

It hardly needs to be said that my parents didn't sleep a wink that night, and for the first time it wasn't my fault!

The next day Dr. Doncel arrived with her daughter, Peggy, a girl like any other, although with one less arm. A mere detail.

Cheerful, with black hair and dark eyes, she greeted my parents—and just then realized something: "Oh, my shoe-laces have come undone," she commented casually. And just like any other girl, with or without a missing arm, she bent down, put one knee on the ground, and tied the laces of her sneakers so skillfully that my parents could not hide their surprise. Even so, neither of them said anything, and neither the doctor nor her daughter seemed to notice my parents' jaws were hanging open.

They spent the rest of the afternoon talking, sharing anecdotes and concerns. Peggy didn't just lead a normal life but was even first in her class, had lots of friends, and had a smile that never left her face, not even when she commented on the bad experiences a person might suffer because of first impressions. Nonetheless, after the scene with the shoelaces, my parents had already seen all they needed. The fact that Peggy had knelt down and tied her shoelaces without any problem meant there was hope that I could be normal, that I could tie my own shoes and even reach NASA (oops, spoiler!). Barely any shadows remained in their vision of my future.

The truth is, it was a simple gesture, almost an absurd one. I'm sure that when you tie your shoes, you do so in an automatic way; you probably haven't thought about it since you first learned how to do it. Same for me. Just like Peggy, I would manage to do it—that and so much more. However, I can imagine why a smile grew on my mother's face and tears welled in my father's eyes on that day so long ago.

During dark times, a single spark can reignite extinguished stars and rekindle broken dreams. Before that moment my parents didn't have anyone who could show them that everything would turn out well, that having only one arm wasn't really a tragedy for their son, that it wouldn't leave me helpless. Peggy showed them with that tiny action.

I PUT ON MY SHOES AND . . .

To this day, after so many years, we continue to see Peggy and Dr. Doncel from time to time. They became an unconditional support for us, especially when I was little, and turned what seemed a mountain impossible to scale into crossable hills, thanks to their advice. I often joked that they knew everything, that they were a kind of unique and rare encyclopedia written just for us: the *Manco*-pedia or the WikiCripple. My mother yelled at me whenever I made jokes like that! She couldn't believe that, as little as I was, I already had that kind of humor. Another thing I did was call the poorly named stump on my right arm *"codoñeca"* or "elbowrist." That part, what would have been my elbow, had everything that would have been on my hand but with interrupted growth. Over lunch or dinner, we could spend hours and hours laughing at such things I said. I guess you aren't surprised, right?

In reality Peggy and her mother were no encyclopedia or any kind of instructional manual for kids without an arm. They were just being what they wished they'd had in their day: some support. Years later Dr. Doncel told us she had canceled her entire schedule that day to be able to meet us, and Peggy confessed the scene with the laces was literally that: a little bit of theater to break the ice, a way to say a lot without saying anything, a life jacket that helped us stay afloat in turbulent and confusing waters. For my parents and grandparents, it was the light on the path of their new life by my side. My maternal *abuelo*, Gilbert, was so moved he had to go out into the hallway to weep with joy, both bitter and hopeful.

I remember when I learned this, I thought, "I hope someday I can do the same thing"—save someone—or at least help them by reaching out a hand. Although my *abuela* was the only one who had already firmly believed it would all work out, the rest of us suddenly became aware that I would be the only one to place any limits on myself—not this tiny, minuscule, insignificant, "defective" detail of my anatomy.

Of course, later the world threw all sorts of obstacles at me. But once you learn that the decision to fight is yours, there's no turning back.

From the moment I learned to tie my shoes, I didn't take off my sneakers.

"Are you sure you don't have any homework for tomorrow?" Mamá asked me one day when I was almost nine years old.

My little sister, Naia, had been born by then. She cut in, "I do, Mamá, lots! I have to draw and watch cartoons and—" Naia always liked to pretend she had homework, just like me.

"No," I answered, interrupting her.

But my mother didn't believe me. "The truth," she said.

"It's the truth. No homework. Can I go to the plaza to play with Álex and Ariadna?" They were my best friends, and I was dying to play soccer in the street with them.

"Really?"

"Yes."

"The whole truth?"

"*Yes!*"

"David, you know that lies—"

"I am not lying! I'm not like you with Papá No—" I stopped myself in time. Luckily my sister was too busy pretending to do homework that she didn't have (and which I did) to hear me almost spoil the secret about Santa Claus (we call him Papá Noel here in Andorra). "I don't have homework, I swear it!" I'm sure the fact that I practically shouted and wrinkled my nose didn't help my mother believe me.

Back in those days, as soon as school let out, we had to go to the travel agency where my mother worked. While she finished up her day, my sister and I played without bothering her, or I busied myself with homework for the next day and my sister drew and constantly distracted me. She loved to imitate me, and even though she won't admit it, she is still trying to copy how cool I am. But the problem at that time wasn't my sister or my mother. It was that I already knew how to tie my laces, and play soccer and basketball, and what's more, I could swim well—I beat everyone all the time! And I was dying to go out there and show them at that very moment.

After staring into my eyes for thirty seconds, which to me seemed like thirty years, she said, "All right, you can go. But I want you back here before seven!"

I hardly gave her time to finish speaking. I was already out the door of the agency before she could say, "You can go." I'd done it! It was the first time I had managed to fool my mother with a little white lie, and I felt like the king of the world. It was my chance to breathe, to run, to leap, to laugh. I might lack one arm, but I had both legs! And to be locked inside all afternoon, with those math problems and science questions, was a real slog. Every morning Álex and Ariadna told me about their games and races in the park. They insisted I had to join them and play so the three of us together could be the best in gym later.

"But if he plays with you two, he's got only one hand to protect himself from your fumbled shots," Jordi, another classmate, had said that morning. He'd overheard us talking in the schoolyard and chose to take a verbal swipe at me, as usual. "You don't even know what scoring a goal is!" And one at my friends, while he was at it.

"Shut up," I told him. But he never closed his mouth. As you'll see. "I plan to play with them this afternoon, big mouth."

Soon after, my friends went off. How was I going to manage this if my mother never took her eyes off me? I could think only of showing the world they were wrong about me, and at nine years old, my world was reduced to school and the latest bully. Take that, Jordi!

But once I arrived at the park and they passed me the ball, the only things that existed were the imaginary goal (the space between the green bench and the one that creaked when you sat on it) and my friends. The wild kicks, the running, the goals . . . I remember that I won. I don't know how, since it was just us three playing, but I won. It was a wonderful afternoon. Jumping and running somewhere that wasn't phys ed class was like a breath of fresh air. Suddenly it was like being on the island of Menorca, where my family always went for holidays: the freedom, the nonstop games, the origami, having fun . . . The only things missing were the scent of the sea and the warm breeze on the beach. It was February, and summer was still so far away, separated from now by endless days of school and tedious hours of homework.

The spell was broken by ringing church bells: they warned us it was almost 6:00 p.m., and it was time for the three of us to go.

Álex and Ariadna grabbed their backpacks, got on their bikes, and disappeared around the corner, heading toward their homes. I admit I felt a certain jealousy about that, not because I didn't know how to ride a bike but because I couldn't. Almost a year earlier I'd started to outgrow my bicycle, and it was no longer comfortable for me to ride. I kept growing, and it was no longer good for me. I definitely couldn't ride it with such ease. Until then I'd been able to lean forward slightly and hold the handlebar with my left hand and the stump, but that position became more and more uncomfortable, until I couldn't even grab the handlebar by bending forward. As a result, some nights I found myself wishing I'd stop growing. Was this what growing up meant? Would I need to stop doing the things I enjoyed? I felt like I was suffocating. It was exhausting having to learn again and again to do the things I'd already learned how to do, just because my body stretched and changed its dimensions.

And at nine years old, I wanted only to ride a bike. I didn't think it was too much to ask for.

When I returned to the travel agency that afternoon, I couldn't imagine what awaited me. My school schedule lay open on my mother's desk. The most accusatory page was staring up at me, at us: a list of homework assignments impossible for me to complete for the next day, incriminating me as only my own confession might have done.

"Peux-tu m'expliquer ce que cela signifie?"

There's something I haven't yet told you about my mother, Nathalie. When she gets very upset, she speaks in French; she reverts to her mother tongue. So you can imagine how much that question made me shrink, especially since my birthday was just a few weeks away. Looking back, I could have chosen a better moment to lie to her and show my friends (and my not-so-friends) everything I could do, but I guess my pride was too strong. That's why—and also not to make things even worse with another lie—I opted for the simple truth: "I wanted to play with my friends, Mami."

She always melts when I call her "Mami." Even today.

I recommend you try it; it's infallible.

Joking aside, I explained everything to her, and to my surprise, her reprimand was a hug.

"You could have told me. And then we would have taken care of your homework. Oh, and I'll have a talk with your teacher about this Jordi, who's starting to be too much of a pest. *Quel imbécile!*"

After that, we gathered our things and Mamá closed the office, but not before telling me, "And don't think you've gotten out of any punishment, young man." There went my birthday presents. "You'll complete all today's homework without any help, and you're not allowed to watch *The Iron Giant!*"

I won't deny that I was very upset not to be able to watch my favorite cartoon, about a robot who built himself and did good for humankind. I felt like the show called to me; it spoke to only me. I also spent a few days without going out to recess, because I hadn't finished all the homework from that day. But at least what I feared most didn't come to pass.

A few days later, on my birthday, my parents gave me something that would wind up being so special for me: a construction set of a LEGO ship. That gift marked a before and after in my life and would become an inspiration for my father, who later composed a fantastic song for my documentary, *Mr. Hand Solo*, titled "Oh, LEGO."

But getting back to that day when I lied to my mother, I remember I went to bed early that night. When she came to tuck me in, a little smirk escaped me, and I couldn't help saying to her, "Mamá, I don't know how you managed to catch me."

She gave me one of the biggest and warmest smiles I've seen in my life.

"David, you need to realize two things. The first is that I was once a little girl myself; I know all the tricks. And the second is that I'm your mother, *chéri*. Where you go, I follow. When you want to spend time with your friends, I'd prefer if you just told me, OK? You need to promise that, from now on, you'll think twice before lying to me, because I'll always catch you."

And that's how it was from then on.

. . . I COULDN'T STAY STILL

Don't get me wrong. It's not as if that ship was my first LEGO set, but with it . . .

I won't get ahead of myself.

As I said, it wasn't my first LEGO set. In fact, it's hard for me to remember what the first was because . . . well, I must've been very little when I got it. How old? Maybe five or perhaps just four. I swear sometimes, as I'm telling you all this, I need to ask my parents about some details. It's strange how memory works. If we think about it, what do we wind up remembering? We've lived days that are such highlights, incredible events that happen just once in a life-time but are stored in our memories only as emotions, very precise and detailed (joy, fear, impatience, shame). Other times we associate what we've lived with colors (how many black days, blue ones, or yellow ones have you managed to have?). And only rarely do events reproduce themselves in our heads one after another, in perfect order, spotless.

In my case, the Oscar for the Best Adaptation of a Memory goes to the first time I rode a bike! My father held the seat. I had my hand on the handlebar, the stump resting on the brakes. I pedaled with all my strength, and my father encouraged me to keep going. It was a yellow afternoon, and I had feelings of happiness and clear images of the trees, the gravel path, and the park of my childhood under the watchful gaze of my grandparents. I remember my father's smile and my own. At last I was riding a bicycle! At last I felt and saw myself like a normal boy.

That memory is complete and replays in my mind like a Netflix movie. I can even choose the language and subtitles. However, other memories are hazy and blurry, and there are even experiences that have completely disappeared, despite being important and crucial for my life. Who could know when I was little that putting together toys would someday lead me to put together a book?

I've always been told that I loved any sort of construction game since I was really little. As I've said, I can barely remember this fact. The only thing that appears in my mind is how much fun I had constructing things (doing so evoked emotions of happiness and joy, the colors orange and yellow). I'd build things all by myself, with just one hand, as well as play with them. First came the little figurines from these chocolate eggs we have here in Europe. Inside the eggs are toy surprises, like little plastic animals riding on motorcycles or bicycles, with instructions for how to assemble them. Every time my parents gave in and got me one of those chocolate eggs I had begged them to buy, I'd tear off the wrapper and throw it in the trash, and the chocolate practically went with it. What I wanted was to reach the little orange capsule that was so difficult to open with the toy inside. I often used my teeth to help get it open and got yelled at for doing so! Since I was so passionate about building things, discovering which toy I'd gotten was one of my biggest thrills. I didn't give my parents the figurine so they'd put it together for me; I gave them the chocolate! For them to eat! And I went crazy putting pieces together, not because it was hard for me but because I loved doing it. Piece by piece, without even looking at the instructions, I built my koala up in a tree, my Smurf in a cap on a bicycle, my pathetic puzzle with just six pieces. (I was always so frustrated and angry when my surprise was a mere puzzle!)

I imagine you must think I'm pulling your leg. What can I tell you? It's all a question of practice. I mean, I didn't put together that first little figure in less than five minutes. But right away I got the hang of it. In fact, I was so skilled at putting them together it would be years before I realized the little piece of paper that showed all the figures from the collection had instructions on the back. I always tossed it along with the wrapper and the chocolate.

Yes, even from the beginning, I built without following the instructions, without rules. Without limits. Today I still do the same, and I don't know how I do it. It's a kind of intuition, as if the pieces tell me where they should go, and the points, flaps, and joints shine precisely where they should be connected. My fingers vibrate, and I feel the emotion and colors, the impulse to create something new from something old. The materials are there, and the essence, too. I give it a new shape, a usefulness, a new meaning that wasn't there before.

It's a composition, I think. *Dum, du-dum-du, dum-du-dum, dum.* And repeat. Sounds that on their own have consistency, form, and color, and together they're recomposed and shape their own sounds and experiences.

Dum.

Du-dum-du.

Dum-du-dum.

Plash.

Dum.

Plash.

Du-dum-du.

Plash, plash.

(I assure you this musical composition sounds much better on my Launchpad than on paper.)

As I said, the pieces are there, but they reach their true meaning only when joined together.

When I opened the gift on my ninth birthday and discovered the LEGO set, I knew what I was going to build: a spectacular ship. I got a thrill just thinking about it. I was really happy, and this is something I don't just remember well; there are photos that offer unquestionable proof (in a very embarrassing way). The pieces that came in the box (all separate, in little bags: black ones, white ones, brown ones, gold ones, little pieces, big pieces, huge pieces) had a goal: for me to put them together one by one to make a fabulous ship that, if I managed to build it properly, wouldn't sink in my bathtub.

I finished in a few days without a single mistake. It was a splendid ship that looked just like the photograph on the box, one James Cameron would be jealous of, especially because his *Titanic* cost many millions of dollars more. Although, I have to say, it was one of the large LEGO boxes, so it was still something my parents felt in their pocketbooks had cost the same.

But in the end I'm not telling you this so you can see how good I am at building LEGOs and everything I can do with five fingers, one and a half arms, plus the stump of my *bracito*. No. What happened is, when I built the ship and saw it was identical to the one on the box, I felt something very different. Of course I felt satisfied at seeing the result—I was very content and ran to show it to my parents and sister. Naia wouldn't stop touching it and almost tore off a mast as if she were some kraken, thereby changing the story of Jack Sparrow forever. But something was missing. For the first time I had put together a LEGO set and then thought, "Now what?"

The pieces, in themselves, have meaning, but together they take on a new meaning: they become a *Titanic*, or Big Ben, or Hogwarts. At the same time, couldn't I build something else with them, aside from a ship? Couldn't I create a new meaning with them? Maybe, just maybe, I could build anything I wanted to try making. Maybe even a prosthetic arm.

That was what I saw when I put the ship on my shelf. It was the first thing I'd built that I left on display on my shelves. Somehow I knew it wasn't the end for that LEGO set, even if it wasn't yet time to make it what it would be.

I know it seems silly, but for me it was a click, like when two LEGO pieces fit together perfectly.

After the games of *rompecuellos*, the bike, and the superbike that came later, and after the clandestine soccer matches when school got out, there came a time when I was tired of hearing the same old story and being looked at in a very specific way, with a mix of pity, shame, and compassion, and sometimes even disgust. And I didn't want to endure it much longer, you know? I didn't want—for even a second—to feel in front of the mirror the way I felt when I walked down the street.

Watched.

Judged.

Pigeonholed.

Manco.

Useless.

Unable.

Damaged.

That wasn't what I wanted to see in the mirror. No.

So I guess that became my first form of rebelling, even before I turned thirteen. Making what I wanted from the pieces.

◆ ◆ ◆

"If you don't stop doing *entremeliadures*, you're going to wind up missing the *colonias*. *D'accord?*" Mamá said one day when I was ten. As I mentioned, my mother slips into French when she gets angry, but she also mixes it with Catalan when she gets nervous. (I can't deny this is perfect to let me know when I'm in *big* trouble.) That time I could tell I wasn't yet in danger of not going on the trip with the rest of my class; but the *"d'accord"* let me know she was really angry. I'd have to be on my best behavior for a few days to not run the risk of being forced to stay home while my friends were learning English, playing sports and games, and having an amazing time.

Back then it wasn't enough for me to ride a bike, get good grades, play soccer, and make model planes; I also liked playing pranks. Álex and Seri joined in without problems, and David and Pep were also always up for any mischief. Literally. In those days spitballs were all the rage. The teachers would barely turn around, and the ceiling would gain another damp lump of paper. With me, the fad lasted maybe two months at most.

If it had been just that, probably nothing more would have happened. Who really cares about four bits of paper on the classroom ceiling? But, of course, things didn't stop there. That day, in one of my attacks on the ceiling, the teacher turned around and caught me with the pen in my mouth.

"David!"

I was so startled I almost swallowed both the piece of paper and the pen.

"I never expected this of you! You, especially, should pay more attention."

The words echoed in my mind.

"You, especially."

"You, especially."

"You, especially."

Of course. Because I'm missing an arm, I thought. In fact, that *especially* was what had made her catch me in flagrante. If I'd had two hands, I could have removed the converted blowpipe from my mouth with one and held a normal pen in the other to pretend I was paying attention. But no. I had one hand, and the teacher had caught me.

If she thought I was *less than* the rest of my classmates, she was very mistaken. And to demonstrate that point, by the end of class her hair was full of little balls of paper. The rest of the kids couldn't stop laughing, and *that* caught her attention.

I, *especially*, had ruined her perm.

"If it ever occurs to you to do something like this again, you won't see your friends again. You'll see. Terrible influences!" My mother reprimanded me for a long while. The scolding I got that afternoon was monumental and lasting.

"But, Mamá . . ."

"No *buts*, David. What your teacher said was not at all right, but neither was what you did. You must respect your teachers!"

"Even if they don't respect me?"

There is no denying I turned out to be argumentative.

Mamá sighed, stroked my cheek, and said, "Things don't function like that, *chéri*. Sometimes you'll have to endure comments like those, and it will take a lot of effort on your part to respond correctly. I'll have a talk with that teacher, don't you worry, but I'm sure she said it without even thinking. In any event, that doesn't excuse you from spitting bits of paper at her! *Petit cochon!* And if you get into more trouble—"

"You can forget about going to the *colonias*," I finished.

Mamá nodded and left me in my room with my homework. Really, I don't think she was mad because I took revenge on my teacher with spitballs. I could tell she was madder at the teacher for undervaluing me. She always encouraged me to defend myself against anyone who tried to mess with me! But, of course, it's not the same thing when it's Jordi as when it's a teacher. Even so, I think what my mother really wanted was for me *not* to go to the *colonias*. It was the first time I'd be going, and she was worried.

But make no mistake, I hadn't passed on going before because they wouldn't let me. On the contrary, I was the one who hadn't felt strong enough to go on the trip before. I was able to do lots of things, but my parents were always at my side in everything I did. I suppose I unconsciously saw them as a safety net, a life vest in case anything turned out badly. If my courage stumbled or waned, they were there. Leaving home, spending a few nights away, entailed not having that safety net and being at the mercy of the teachers—and even worse, of my classmates! I didn't want them to see that I could fail and confirm all their prejudices about my abilities. That terrified me much more than the damage I could do to myself if, say, I fell from a zip line or off a pony. I didn't just fear the mockery from Jordi, Marc, and Samuel, or the pitying looks from Carles, Marina, and the teacher, but also my own gaze. Would I dare to do the things the world told me I couldn't? Or would the fear of failing paralyze me?

But with fear we are nothing.

We must fight against fear, overcome the obstacles, visualize them, and leap over them. And if we fail, if we fall from a pony or from a zip line, we pick ourselves up, tend our wounds, learn from the errors we made, and try again.

Until it turns out right.

I know this now, but when you're ten, you neither know nor understand this. You leap into the void, crash against the fear, and freeze, wondering if you should keep going or if it's better to throw in the towel.

As I said, my parents didn't forbid me to "leap into the void," so I didn't let fear forbid me, either. Whenever I saw myself capable, I took the leap I needed to take in that moment. And right then, the pool waiting for me to dive into it was *las colonias*. Later, an excursion in a kayak or on the new bike, learning to drive . . .

But let's not get ahead of the events (maybe I should be more careful with the spoilers).

I have fantastic memories from those days at the *colonias*: I rode a pony without falling off, I went down the zip line shouting with the thrill, and I played soccer with my friends until I collapsed onto my bunk bed at night (the upper one, of course). What's more, if I hadn't gone to those *colonias*, I surely wouldn't have gone to the later ones, which were so special for me.

To be fair, I have to let you know I didn't always have good times.

Not always, after leaping from the diving board, is the splash clean and triumphant. Sometimes when you dive you stumble on the edge of the pool, and, well, how do you recover from that?

Worst thing of all, it might happen at any time.

A DAY LIKE
ANY OTHER

R eally, it was.

A day like any other, I mean. We have to leap forward in time, OK? What I'm going to tell you now took place just a few years ago, when I went to my first year of *bachillerato*, which is like the final years of high school in the United States. And it really was a day like any other. I promise. I swear it. It wasn't raining cats and dogs, nor even *bots i barrals*, as we say in Andorra, where I'm from; the sun wasn't shining, the birds weren't sing-ing, no melancholy snow had begun to fall. Although, I guess the birds did sing, but I didn't hear them. My mind was on other things: the scooter I wanted to fix, my chemistry test, a golden ocean full of prepositions with two green lighthouses that . . .

Oh, yes, sorry. I was going to talk about the weather. The sky was cloudy; it had the gray tone of a bored day. Of a day like any other. But in reality it wasn't, because I was walking to school, thinking about how to fix my scooter, with a secret locked in my mind that left my chest vibrating. Today would be very different because I had made a decision: I was going to tell Marta I liked her.

There was nothing really special about that: a boy liked a girl, and the boy worked up the courage to tell her. The same old story as always.

I'd put on my favorite T-shirt, tucked the sleeve of the shirt I wore over it into my pants pocket so it didn't dangle, and wore for the first time the new sneakers I'd gotten for my birthday. I was going to ask her on a date at last, and a guy had to be ready, right? It had to be a unique and different moment. Marta and I had already chatted for hours and hours by WhatsApp—and not just about schoolwork, exactly! The time had come for us to have dinner and go to the movies, and for me to tell her how I felt about her.

Or at least that's what I thought.

But careful, no spoilers. Don't let me get ahead of myself.

On the way to school, I ran into Álex, and after the usual foolishness, I couldn't hold back anymore. I told him about my plan.

"Man, you're crazy." That's the only thing he could say to me, but he said it with a laugh—and if your friends laugh at the madcap things you're planning to do, that means they're a good kind of madness.

Besides, he was right. I was crazy. Not because I was missing an arm, but because Marta was just too much. Let me explain a few things to you.

Marta was pretty, so very pretty. That's the short explanation. The longer one is: Marta had green eyes like two lamps, a golden cascade of hair that left all the girls in town asking her what shampoo she used, and a head for language and literature that made her hypnotic to listen to. Marta was a siren of syntax; she loved prepositions and adverbs. Just as I handled cables and LEGOs, she handled words. And that drove me crazy. Like really crazy. I can't deny it. So I guess I *was* crazy, but not in the sense Álex meant.

"Crazy as a loon," I answered, "but aren't my sneakers cool?"

He gave me a slap on the back, and we kept walking. Little did I know what I would find in class.

"Hey, David," Jordi greeted me when I arrived. I've already told you he's been on my case from the beginning. I was surprised he'd say hello, because he was usually a jerk to me. "Can you lend me *a hand* with the math homework?" he asked, stretching out his right hand.

As you can see, it took 0.7 seconds for him to act like usual—that is to say, like a complete and total bonehead.

With all I've been telling you, I think it's pretty clear I've never been too popular. Just then I stood there staring at him.

"Oh, sorry!" Some giggles could be heard from our classmates. "I guess I have the upper *hand* on this one." And the chuckles broke out.

It's hard to believe that people still get on your case or sell you short, even if you do great things. Jordi had been in my class when I'd built the first prosthesis; he knew what I was capable of. Although, come to think of it, I haven't yet told you about that. But what I want to explain now is: I barely cared at all about his opinion. One of the biggest lessons you need to learn in this life is that reaching your goals, whatever they are, is what's important—but you need to do it for yourself.

"No. You'd actually need to have a brain for that."

I won't tell you about the look he gave me just then. Because right at that moment the teacher came into the classroom, and immediately everyone sat down. Once at my desk, I pulled out my phone to see if Marta had responded to my messages from that morning. I had sent her a note about meeting up later at school. She hadn't written back. Just then I couldn't see anything else, only *that*—that she hadn't answered me. I thought she must be busy or maybe her class had started already. And if I wasn't able to interpret her silence, then how could I have realized her texted smileys were grimaces and her friendship was instead pity? Or that her friends were looking at me and elbowing one another?

So at recess I jumped in and wrote her again on WhatsApp. Then came two eternal hours until it was time for lunch. I couldn't stop thinking of how to approach her, write her, ask her, invite her to dinner. I would begin with the easy part.

That day the hallways seemed infinite to me, the doors were heavier than usual, and my legs felt stiff with each step. At that precise moment, no matter how I'd dared to leap into the void on other occasions, I suddenly discovered it was hard to work up the courage. Sitting there, separated by a screen, I finally took a deep breath and typed:

Will you go to dinner with me sometime?

She read it right away; I saw the check mark turn blue in less than a second. What I couldn't see was that she stopped smiling as soon as she looked at her phone.

I left it that we could write more after classes to coordinate the details.

I felt dizzy for the rest of the day. When I was little, I fantasized about piloting helicopters. I liked them so much people started to give me not just LEGOs as gifts but toy choppers, too, and I hurried to put them together as I had never hurried before with those cars or buildings, the little figurines from the chocolate eggs. I even dreamed I piloted them and surfed the skies without any limits, imagining what it must feel like to fly them. I thought it had to be similar to what I was feeling just then: a gentle dizziness as if my head were in the clouds—because I really had it in the clouds! But now that I stop to think about it, that afternoon was more like if I'd climbed into a washing machine and turned on the full spin cycle.

In any event, that day the sky was cloudy, I was dizzy, and Marta finally answered me with monosyllables. I don't know how I didn't see it coming:

No.

It was an important blow. Like a helicopter accident.

No?

No, David. I don't want to have dinner with you.
Ka-pow.

As I've already said, I hadn't noticed many things that day, but, boy, could I tell Marta wanted to add something more.

I don't want to *go out with you.*
And, boy, did she add it; she even wrote it in italics.

But why not?
Maybe, just maybe, I should have bitten my tongue and not asked, just like I was resisting my urge to kick and scream like a toddler. But something told me I needed to know. Although what I didn't know yet was that it would change my life.

We have a good time together, right?

Yes, but . . .
Marta was doing it again: she wanted to add something more, but she didn't release it. It was like the words were getting stuck in her throat. She must have had a knot that was tighter than the one in my own. Oh, if only she'd

swallowed those words instead of spitting them out like an ugly buckshot of truth laced with venom.

But you're missing an arm. And . . .

She wrote me a lot of things. That, yes, she had a good time with me, but "it" (my arm, or lack of an arm) gave her "the creeps." That her friends "laughed at her" (no, Marta, they laughed at *me*; maybe now you understand better), and she just "couldn't." That she felt bad. That we were friends. That she hoped I forgave her.

Without knowing how, I managed to say goodbye and archive the chat without blocking her.

Returning home, I felt like the stupidest creature on the face of the earth. Despite her words through a cold mobile phone screen, at that moment I didn't feel like I was missing an arm but instead a damned brain. Did I really think she wouldn't realize? That she wouldn't keep it in mind? Maybe that's why I had debuted my sneakers, to distract and fool myself. They were white, shiny, like the stupid truth. They were as noticeable as reality, as that extremity I was missing—which was the only thing people could see of me. Whatever I did, whatever I achieved, whether for myself or them, that was the only thing they could manage to see.

How was this possible? I was so much more than that.

I was more than an absence.

I *am* more than a lack.

"David?" my mother called when she heard the door slam.

Before I could explain anything to her, her tone was already one of concern; not just because a slammed door is usually a bad sign but also because back then I told her everything. So from the moment Marta's smile bewitched me for the first time, my mother knew how crazy I was for this girl.

"Do you think I should tell her how I feel?" I had asked her the night before. Often, when Marta went silent in our conversations on WhatsApp, I went to my mother for advice. I knew she could advise me better than anyone. Well, really I knew that after the first two times I asked my mother and saw her advice worked. It's not like I didn't know what to talk about with Marta or that we had nothing in common; the pieces just didn't always fit, and I needed to consult the instruction manual so the whole construction didn't collapse.

It took me a while to understand that, if the conversation resembles Jenga more than LEGO, perhaps there's no foundation on which to build anything.

"Like, a formal declaration?" my mother had asked, perplexed. "You're not going to propose marriage to her, are you?"

I'd shrugged. Wasn't that supposed to be romantic?

"Isn't that supposed to be romantic?" I'd had to extract that thought from my head.

"It's one thing for you to be romantic and quite another to be too serious."

I couldn't help wrinkling my brow. Were feelings always going to be so difficult? It was usually so easy to put things together, but now . . .

"I thought romanticism implied seriousness."

"You just need to loosen up a bit. *Soit courageux!* Instead of doing it so formally, invite her to dinner or the movies. Marta will understand you want to go out with her without needing you to ask her parents for her hand."

But, of course, as soon as she heard the way I slammed the door, I'm sure she knew *mon courage* had shattered against the ground and broken into a thousand pieces.

Ignoring both my parents, I went up to my room, climbing the steps like I'd never done before: first two steps at a time and then three. I locked myself in my bedroom and lay on the bed, thoughtful and sad and above all completely disillusioned. I spent hours alone there, without looking at anything, wondering why real life wasn't easier and, especially, fairer. At one moment I raised my gaze and saw the flamboyant red-and-yellow LEGO helicopter that had been gathering dust there for years. My mother always asked me to clean it or do something with it. Maybe she was sending me some kind of sign? Heavyhearted, I remembered how I'd built a prosthetic with the LEGO from the ship my parents had given me when I turned ten. I remained frozen there, staring at the helicopter, then stood up to grab it. I barely left my room for five long days.

I had made another decision that, without knowing it, would change my life.

FALL DOWN AND
. . . GET BACK UP?

Don't think I've forgotten my own advice. If you fall, you tend your wounds, get back up, and try again. But try to do all that when you've just had the biggest blow of your life. Try to do it when you've fallen down three flights of stairs, one after another, or when, after leaping from the diving board, the clean dive winds up being a true belly flop, or when the parachute doesn't open and the flop, instead of being on the water and just stinging a lot, is on the tarmac and leaves you like a fried egg.

That was how I was at that moment: a fried egg.

With a bit of salt and pepper.

And fried potatoes on the side.

Because, as every chef knows, fried eggs aren't served on the plate alone.

Well, neither are disgraces.

I didn't realize then, but looking back, as I'm retelling all this for you, I can see how my happiness and everything I'd worked on with my parents and alone after going off to the *colonias* just . . . deflated, like a soufflé, right then.

I'm going to get very hungry if I keep making these food similes.

Little by little I had lost strength. The *rompecuellos* game stopped having an effect: their gazes felt sharper, I would say even more personal, as if it bothered people I was missing an arm; and pity became disgust that I read not just in their gazes but also in the grimaces I saw twisting the lips of those whose paths crossed mine. *Penasco* (that mix of pity and disgust) falls short to describe what I thought people felt on seeing me. For me, what I saw in their faces was the most absolute repugnance. After that it was impossible to turn and catch them looking at me. I didn't want to know if they turned around to look at me and verify that, yes, I was missing an arm, and yes, they had seen right: half the sleeve of my coat was cut off.

For a long time, since I was born, my mother had tailored all the clothes she bought me so I didn't need to go around with one sleeve dangling. Long-sleeved T-shirts, polo shirts, sweaters, sweatshirts, hoodies, jackets, coats. Everything with a long sleeve—snip, *chas-chas-chas*—passed through her scissors and sewing machine. It was Abuela Basi who began this tradition when she realized the clothes she dressed me in didn't fit me well; one thing was the swaddling cloth she'd knitted, a small blanket that worked in any event, but the onesies she had bought me? She couldn't bear to see the extra bit of fabric dangling from the little arm, so she set to work with a needle and thread. In a single afternoon, all my baby clothes were altered.

"Come, Nathalie, let me show you."

Thus, my mother learned from my *abuela* to make these kinds of alterations, so between the two of them, they made my life easier.

For an ordinary person, clothes are nothing more than whatever they put on every day to go outside, a few scraps of fabric they keep in a closet that's more or less in order. For some of us, they are something more: a means by which to feel safe, a way of expressing personality, or a pile of treasures. For me, those altered pieces were my superhero outfit. Every item was made especially for me, adapted to my body, my anatomy, my absence. For many years, when I put on those pieces, I felt like Spider-Man when he puts on his first outfit, the one he makes himself. Enthusiastic. Euphoric. Unique.

Free.

In short, I felt like myself.

And at the same time, I thought I was like everyone else; I had clothes that fit me. Wasn't this what a person with two arms felt like when they put on a shirt with two sleeves?

But, of course, mine had a sleeve and a half. And although I loved that, to other people it continued to be surprising or even strange. I might think I was Spider-Man, but the world around me seemed determined to make me feel a bit like spotting Superman flying by: *Is it two arms? Is it one? No, it's one and a half!* The altered sleeve was my cape, and I felt invincible with it.

"Look, David," Álex said, elbowing me when we got off the bus at the main house on our trip to the *colonias* during the second year of ESO, the final year of required secondary education (like tenth grade in the United States).

Remember I told you these *colonias* were very special ones?

Down the same highway that had led us there came a blue double-decker bus that clearly belonged to a different transportation company from the one we were on. That could mean only one thing.

"Wow, we're going to be with another school?" I asked, surprised.

"The teachers haven't said anything . . ."

"What nerve," I said. "They could have warned us."

If I had dared to go to the *colonias* with my friends, my classmates, my teachers, it was because of precisely that—they were "mine." Don't worry, I'm not going to start meditating on demonstrative possessives the way I did with prepositions; I just want you to understand me. I dared to try new things with *my* classmates, *my* world, not with others'. And suddenly I found myself trapped in a house with strangers. That was a challenge I hadn't signed up for, a pool I didn't want to dive into.

It was hard to trust myself in front of people I knew and who knew me. No matter how much Jordi got on my case, he knew the panorama perfectly: he knew my situation, my family knew his family, and we went to the same school. We all knew what to do, the lines we shouldn't cross. But with strangers, things weren't like that at all. With strangers everything was new, and for me it was like starting over. The stares. The lack of understanding. The disgust. The pity. A few necks broken from the melodramatic twisting of heads. Or from shame when they became aware of their crass error and lack of manners.

I was tired of all that. For many it would seem I'm missing an arm, but in reality its weight rests on my shoulders. It's like I'm always carrying a backpack that by itself is heavy. I already carry my own "books," but people insist I bear the weight of theirs as well, and their books have different but always long titles. The main bestsellers are:

How to Lose an Arm in Nine Months of Gestation

Living without an Arm: The Original Trilogy

Stumps: Everything You Need to Know about Them

Things You Think You Can't Do without an Arm (but Can)

How to Stare without Acting Like Someone Rude but Still Being Rude

A Manco Who Ties His Shoes

And I'll give you a spoiler: those "books" are very heavy! Back then I wound up carrying twice or even three times the weight, so it wasn't just my own thoughts running around my head and sapping my energy but also those of everyone else. While I didn't have to bear their burdens, my mind absorbed them and made them my own. They mingled with my own, and I devoured them and turned them into a new thing, until even I didn't know anymore whether they belonged to me. Had I created them, as if I were a kind of Dr. Frankenstein, or had they been created by others in the image and likeness of what they thought they saw in me, like a horde of angry townsfolk?

In short, on those days, during those *colonias*, I didn't feel like carrying anyone's "books," or being Superman, or battling with my own thoughts inside my head. For once I decided not to exhaust myself with the prejudices of others. What I did was to pull bravery and strength from my yearning to have a good time with my friends. I was determined to grab the bull by the horns, even if I had to do it with just one arm.

"Class!" the teacher called. "What do you say we welcome the girls and boys who will share this dormitory with us for the next three days?"

We all broke into cheers of one kind or another. Many of my classmates let loose a resounding *"Yes!,"* completely excited by the possibility of making new friends or facing off against new rivals in long games of soccer or basketball. Others were content to offer a shy, "Yes," a bit terrified at being with kids they didn't know.

And me?

I laughed. Because I had thought of the perfect welcome.

"What are you laughing about?" Álex asked, a bit confused.

Although at first he had been taken aback when he'd seen the other bus, the idea of sharing the house with new people had excited him more than he dared to admit; in the end, he'd been one of the ones who'd shouted most enthusiastically. It didn't surprise me, nor did it even bother me. I knew how much he liked to play soccer. Me too. And couldn't I enjoy myself just as much as everyone else? Would I have to let their "books" spoil my time during the *colonias*?

I'd save myself from all their questions with a single blow. With a single gesture.

Before the bus parked alongside ours, I put both arms behind my back, as if I were the only boy of the whole excursion who had never broken a plate in his entire life. Soon after, the bus stopped before us, and the kids from the other school started to disembark, as surprised and animated to find themselves with us as we had been when we learned the news.

My classmates smiled and welcomed them. Then I discovered my arm and a half. I shook my arms and started to bray like a madman while sticking out my tongue. Their faces were the best combination of surprise and horror I'd seen in my life. Some fell on their butts, others took off running, and a few jumped back onto the bus, begging to be taken home. And then there were the teachers who didn't know what to do, and also the bus driver, who clutched the steering wheel as if he'd seen the very Phantom of the haunted *colonias*.

The laughter of my classmates, who were just cracking up, mingled with the shouts of the students from the other school and blurred together. I joined their cackles even before I stopped playing the clown. I couldn't hold back anymore, and laughter bubbled up in me, freeing me from the weight that had been pressing down on my shoulders since the moment I'd first seen their bus.

Almost right away the teachers from the other school understood the situation, and mine realized what I'd done all by myself. The laughs stopped sooner for me than for anyone, but when they sat me down in front of the teachers of both schools and I crossed my arms, everyone understood very quickly why I had decided to put on that little show. And no, it wasn't because I'd suddenly discovered an aspiration to become a horror-movie director.

It was because I was fed up, and I wasn't going to put up with any more.

The world needed to know I was more than a cripple, a *manco*, a wreck, an absence. I was rebellious, funny, fun, clever. I was David.

With or without my altered sleeves.

Yes, if I fell, I got back up. If they cried with pity on seeing me, I answered with laughter.

Until I couldn't pull any more strength from my weakness. Until I couldn't even make jokes. That's the problem with trying to grab the bull by the horns; if your arm fails in the end, you might wind up getting skewered by those very horns.

As if they were an oasis, during those *colonias*, I dared to do everything, and I had a fabulous time. For a few days I thought that everything would work out well, that I would always be on the crest of the wave, being the special and unique boy I wanted to be and was. I managed to integrate after my little prank, and in the end, I wound up spending a great few days, among the best in my life.

But in oases there are neither water currents nor waves. An oasis is a quiet space, calm and peaceful, frozen in time. Oases are special and unique places, yes, but also ephemeral.

Everything went well for a while after that, until those glances that had always fallen on me began to follow me like never before. I didn't want to be a horror-movie director and even less to direct slasher films and spend my life running. As quickly as that confidence had been born during those fleeting moments at the *colonias*, soon I began to want to fit into the mold others had always wanted to put me into. I asked my mother to stop altering my clothes for me, with the goal of not feeling special and unique, not being different.

In reality the only thing I wanted was to fit in, to be like everyone else.

That was becoming more and more difficult with each passing year.

THE DETONATORS

When I was nine years old, Dr. Doncel, who had become my pediatrician, gave us some advice we began to follow as soon as we could: I needed to swim to balance my right pectoral muscle, which was growing asymmetrically with respect to the left. That's what her daughter, Peggy, had done; she'd even become the swimming champion of Andorra and Catalunya. Little by little we settled into a routine: school, homework, swimming, dinner—and building things with LEGO before bed!

But not everything was going to be so easy. The muscle didn't develop as it should.

Before continuing with the story of my thoracic musculature, let me tell you an anecdote so you'll understand me better. During one *verbena* of San Juan, a few years ago

I think—I would have been eighteen already—one of my friends said we needed a detonator for the fireworks.

"A what?" I asked, puzzled but with a smile already on my lips.

"A detonator," he answered as if it were the most natural thing in the world.

"Like Wile E. Coyote and the Road Runner?" another guy asked.

"No, not that. A detonator," he said, completely convinced. "To detonate the fireworks."

"What you want is to blow off the one arm I have," I exclaimed, cracking up.

"Kaboom!" my friend shouted, and only then did he realize he'd mixed up detonators with lighters.

Imagine lighting a firework with a detonator. You connect the cables to the lever, and at the other end is the firework. I don't want you to imagine a Roman candle or rocket; no, nothing that logical. Imagine a sparkler or even a little snapper. Now wouldn't that be absurd? It would be like killing flies with a flamethrower; you'd do it, but you'd also take out half your house. It wouldn't be very useful, right?

Anyway, I'll stop with the anecdotes and get back to what I was telling you.

We went to visit a doctor about my lack of musculature I mentioned before.

"The situation is," the doctor said, talking to my parents two years after Dr. Doncel's suggestion, after I'd been swimming without stopping for more than two years, "your son, David, has Poland syndrome. He will never, ever develop the right pectoral muscle." What tact.

That doctor must have thought a flamethrower wasn't enough to kill flies; let's level up and kill a mosquito with a combat tank, right, Doc?

To have to hear, at twelve, you are more deformed than you already thought (since people have been putting that idea in your head little by little, with their looks, comments, imperceptible gestures that weigh more than any backpack full of books) is not an appetizing dish to eat. Not even a lousy one. It's not even a plate; it's a brick straight to your head, getting hit on the back with a chair, kicked in the shins. And a blow for my parents, too.

I was twelve when I began to feel terrible back pains. Every day it was harder to do simple things, including putting together my beloved LEGOs or continuing to practice the guitar. I didn't much like playing it, but Papá wanted to teach me, and I didn't refuse. I wasn't going to lose the chance to play the guitar and be able to impress girls. But whatever I did—bending forward to bring two pieces together, playing some chords, or doing my homework—became a significant effort, which wound up intensifying the pain I constantly felt in my back.

At first the pains didn't frighten me. They didn't even worry me; I simply thought I was pushing myself too much, that I'd gone past my limits, and since I can be so stubborn, I didn't realize it. Soccer, basketball, and English after school, model planes on weekends, my homework every day . . . I didn't stay still because I didn't want to let my fears become reality; I didn't even want to think of them. If I didn't think of them, they didn't exist—or that's what I wanted to believe, no matter that my worst nightmare had stopped living in my head and had materialized every morning and every afternoon at the door of my house. When I went to school and when I came back, I found it in the entry, glaring at me accusingly, as if I were guilty of everything that was happening. There, beside the garage door, was my bike coated in dust, reminding me of everything I could no longer do—and everything I might stop being able to do.

"*Cariño*, maybe . . . you'll have to cut back on your activities," my mother suggested, holding out the electric blanket for me. I had asked for it as soon as I finished my homework. Luckily that January night was a cold one, and ingenuously I thought I'd get out of talking about my pain by asking for the blanket, using the cold as an excuse.

It didn't work. And what's more, I got angry.

"I don't do too much!" I lied dryly and with sass.

"You do too many extracurricular activities," she insisted even as she tucked the electric blanket around me. Her French accent had suddenly become stronger. My tone was making her angry.

"I don't!"

I couldn't stand for my nightmares to become reality and blend with my life. David, the unmoving. That wasn't going to happen. I didn't want it to happen, with or without back pains, even if I felt the exhaustion in every one of my bones.

I raised my voice so much (OK, fine, I admit it, I *shouted*) my sister, who was in the living room doing her homework (this time for real) turned around to see what was happening. My mother half closed her eyes, and when I went to grab the blanket she had been holding out to me, she pulled it back.

"David, *écoute-moi*! Listen to me. If you don't slow down, the pains are only going to get worse, do you understand? You do too much!"

"Mami is right. You no longer even play with me," my little sister complained. She sure picked a great moment to butt in! I was about to answer her when my mother's glare stopped me. If I dared say anything bad to her little girl

. . . game over, man. To begin with, because Naia didn't deserve it but also because even though I was growing up, we were still inseparable. Would I get anything from taking it out on my little sister in my personal battle to not leave my hobbies behind?

Maybe what I should have done at that moment was be sincere and talk about my fear of turning into someone useless, of never being like Peggy or like the great rally driver Albert Llovera, who came to be a champion in his wheelchair (a poster of him hung in my bedroom for many years). Both of them, Peggy and Albert, had been able to forge ahead, to move forward with ease. But how could I trust I'd be able to do the same, if already I could no longer ride a bike, if the basketball constantly escaped from my hands? But I was terrified to open my mouth. How could I explain to my parents this fear that gripped me? Did my thoughts make any sense? Would it worry them more than it should? But I think my biggest fear was that, in verbalizing it, it would become real.

"I like all the things I do," I said finally, going down a tangent. "I don't want to give up anything."

At that moment Papá arrived home from work, carrying an enormous bag from the hardware store. It was full of metallic bits, rubber, and black leather that poked out the top. He'd been bringing home this kind of stuff for a few weeks now to work on over the weekend. What he did when he arrived home was stuff it all away in his studio in front of the garage, which back then he used as a workshop, and he didn't give us any explanations no matter how often we asked, thinking that a "you'll see" would satisfy our curiosity.

"What's going on?" he asked when he saw Mamá and me facing off over the electric blanket. "Did I miss anything? Does the blanket spark or something?"

"It's that our son is as pigheaded as you!"

My mother wasn't wrong (you must admit it, Papá; we're both very headstrong, although I think what actually happens is that we don't back down for anything).

I got even more upset, but I settled for just huffing and crossing my arms.

"Is it because of his back?"

Papá put an arm around my shoulder, gently, no doubt afraid to hurt me if he was too brusque.

Mamá explained the situation to him, a bit unsettled, mixing French, Spanish, and Catalan as if they were all one language. Luckily we all understood her well. That night I thought she exaggerated a lot and that she should have studied geology, because she was really good at making a grain of sand into a whole mountain, but now I realize she was just really worried. Her fears came before the new diagnosis, and she was convinced my pains were due to my arm, the one I was missing, which was finally causing problems now that I had begun to grow more.

If I had dared to speak about my uncertainties, perhaps we might have saved ourselves that visit to that doctor.

"Maybe it's best if we take you to see a doctor, don't you think, David? I'll look for the best traumatologist to help us," my father suggested with the best of intentions.

"If we have to, we'll leave Andorra. We can go down to Barcelona. They have a larger pool of doctors and . . ." My father continued, but I stopped listening. My heart was beating faster and my vision blurred; the kitchen lost its clarity, and I no longer even remembered the blanket. A doctor could make my nightmares real.

And, as I've said, that's exactly what that Barcelona traumatologist did. Poland syndrome? What was that? Imagine I'm seated in a chair, wearing thick plastic glasses and a white doctor coat, because I'm going to get technical. Ready? Dr. Aguilar enters the room, much more delicate than a respectable traumatologist but with much less knowledge, of course.

Poland syndrome is a rare characteristic from birth (there are pages online that call it a "defect," but there is no defect in any body, however different it might be from normal, which is nothing more than normative) that manifests as the absence or underdevelopment of the pectoral muscle on one side of the body. That is to say, it could be in the right or the left pectoral but not in both. Or at least there are no documented cases of that, anyway. Of course, this characteristic can accompany other diverse formations in the body (again, you've read the term *malformations* about this, but if my body is malformed, that of a "normal" person is as well, because I remind you it's missing an eleventh finger). Out of these formations, we discuss an unusual development of the ribs, dextrocardia, or upper member of the same side of the pectoral affected by the syndrome. And here is where I'd fall: lack of right pectoral muscle with underdevelopment of the upper extremity—in my case, the right arm.

Now I'm going to take off the black plastic glasses for a few minutes. At first glance, and without knowing me well, it looks like I'm completely missing half an arm, but that's not so. My *muñón* is not completely round and smooth; around where the elbow would be, the stump, which begins there, takes on a shape that resembles a tiny hand that's barely formed and from which spring two tiny protuberances I use the same way an ordinary person would use two fingers. It's with them that I manage to tie my shoes, play the guitar, play music on my Launchpad, move LEGO pieces, and so on. In the end it's not a matter of having everything necessary but of doing everything necessary with what you have—of not letting any lack or absence get the upper hand. (That's a good one, isn't it?)

So when I was twelve, almost by pure accident, we discovered that not only am I missing an arm, but what's more I'm missing a pectoral—speaking, of course, in the terms of a world in which there are anatomies that are more valid than others. I began to wonder if I might also be missing a nose. Maybe they took it away when I was little and never gave it back.

I'd never noticed any problem until that day. I'd never observed any physical defect in my body until then. We thought I had a "normal" chest. It might also be that suddenly my nose wasn't a nose. I'd never seen anything strange in the mirror. Nor had my parents when they'd dressed me when I was little. The doctors' explorations had always been positive, and X-rays had never been necessary.

My father, almost more angry than nervous because of the doctor's rudeness, couldn't understand how something like that might have gone unnoticed. "It might take you by surprise," the doctor said. "But it's common for males to have a late diagnosis because it's not so noticeable. In women it affects the development of the mammaries and, of course . . . But in a male it isn't diagnosed until he grows much more and the malformation is noticed aesthetically or rather . . ."

Until you start to have back pains. Let me explain. (Wait, I'll put the glasses back on. Ready.) Because of the lack of the pectoral muscle, the weight this tissue should bear is instead carried by the back, which compensates the force of the muscle that's not there. If it bears too much weight, it starts to hurt. To resolve this ache and avoid it becoming a chronic pain, the patient must fortify the back muscle so as to be able to live with complete normality and do all physical activity that requires effort without any consequences. What happens is that now it might not just affect me during sports but also while doing more banal activities, like leaning over my desk or even carrying my school backpack. I'm sure you're not surprised that the "books" strangers made me carry bothered me so much, right?

"But, Doctor," my mother interrupted, "our son does a lot of sports. Shouldn't that have helped him in this?"

"What sports does he do?"

We explained about the swimming, but it seemed I'd have to swim even more.

It was as if a slab had fallen on top of me, completely ruining my shoulders, back, and all the muscles in my body, both the developed and the underdeveloped. If only I were actually steamrollered, I thought, sitting in the office of that traumatologist, seated between my parents while my mother grabbed my hand very tightly, thinking we could fix something like this, that what she would break with her squeezing was the slab, not my will.

Life, my own body, was snatching everything away from me: I couldn't ride a bicycle, I shouldn't play soccer or basketball, and I'd have to visit a physiotherapist twice a week to undo the muscle contractions so much activity had produced. I couldn't even do my homework quietly, or enjoy the sports I liked, or play with my friends in the park in the afternoon. In addition to the physiotherapy, I had to practice professional swimming, with an even more demanding routine.

When the doctor recommended it to us, the pain in my back rose out of control up to my head, making me feel swollen like a hot-air balloon, and a thick, uncomfortable heat began to spread throughout my body as if it were poisonous water. I didn't know what was happening to me just then, because it was the first time I felt rage at such a level. Yes, my parents had sometimes punished me unjustly, and yes, two or three times my sister had destroyed my LEGO creations by playing with them (without my even having given her permission!). But there is no punishment that lasts for a hundred years or a LEGO construction that can't be fixed or put back together. The rage I'd felt with those childish tantrums was nothing compared to what I felt just then. Where did that fury come from?

How did this doctor think I could practice swimming? Strike that. Fine, I'll do it.

Where did this doctor think I could practice professional swimming? In a municipal sports center? In a gymnasium? Where everyone would stare at me? "Look, it's the cripple come to splash in the water," I could already imagine them thinking. It's one thing to go to the beach, the sea, to spend the summer on Menorca, where I'm happy with my family and quiet, and people splash in the water, or toast in the sun, or drowse under the umbrellas. It's quite a different thing to go to a sports center full of strangers with normal bodies ready to break their backs with their training routines, strangers with perfectly developed motor capacities, skillful and valid.

It was inconceivable for me to go to a gym. Every solution I could think of for my situation crashed against a wall and stopped me from breathing. No one there wouldn't understand. I felt ashamed to swim if it wasn't summer or we weren't at the beach. I felt like everyone was watching me! The rage that surged within me stopped me from reacting to anything else being said in that damned office. So I just said the one thing I felt capable of saying: "I want to go home."

To take a break from everything.

To forget about my body.

Underdeveloped, wrecked, deformed.

Those words headlined the festival held every day in my mind.

I was the image used to illustrate Wikipedia articles dedicated to malformations and strange developments.

Luckily my father, who's very clever, hit on a solution to improve my swimming exercises in the pool we built at home soon thereafter.

I had reached a point at which not even I could believe I was normal. I needed to stop fooling myself. I would never be normal; my absence would always precede me. I wouldn't even be "David, who's missing an arm" and instead was condemned to be "that guy who's missing an arm, David." From then on there were no more sewing machines and no long sleeves shortened and tailored in my life. Now the sleeve hung free, alive, from my right arm, and I stuck the cuff into the pocket of my pants, or my jacket, or my coat. If I stuck my hand in the left pocket, I looked like the usual introverted kid who kept his valuables in his jeans. In short, I started to do what any preadolescent and adolescent did to survive: camouflage myself. Fitting in stopped meaning standing out and being unique. Fitting in began to mean just that: making myself so small I could slip between two Tetris pieces and make the whole column disappear. As much as I might want to touch the sky with the fingers of a hand I didn't have, at that time I thought the best thing would be to fly low to the ground unnoticed. I wanted only to be "normal," whatever that word meant.

But I wasn't going to be let off the hook that easily.

"Hey, *manco*!" Jordi shouted at me at recess, throwing a ball right at me. I managed to step out of the way and catch it. It hadn't been even two weeks since I'd started going to the physiotherapist, and my parents were looking for a solution to the question of swimming. Hearing Jordi made my blood boil, of course. He put effort into making my life impossible, I guess because he was bored.

"What did you call me?" I asked, throwing the ball back at him with my arm. He didn't expect me to be able to throw it with so much force; he took a step back in order to stop it with his hands. It'd been aimed right at his stomach.

"Manco!" he shouted. "Or are you deaf as well?"

He cracked up all by himself. I pretended like I was leaving, but then he sneaked up behind me without my realizing it and shook my little arm, grabbing it with just his thumb and index finger. As if it disgusted him.

"As if you don't see it every day!" he added, shaking it. "Don't go blind now, hey?"

I threw myself at him. In the traumatologist's office I didn't know how to react, nor could I. What could I have done? Give the doctor a wallop? Yeah, right. But I could give Jordi a thrashing. I could even break his face in.

"Enough!" One teacher grabbed me, while another pulled that imbecile from me. "Don't think we didn't see what just happened," he said, talking to Jordi. "You're to go right to the director's office with your tutor. And you, David . . ."

I couldn't even defend myself. They'd come to protect me. I wasn't a violent kid; in fact, that was the refrain of the teacher who separated me from Jordi. He told me it wasn't right to react that way. That I couldn't lower myself to his level, that . . .

I stopped listening. It was all too much for me. I was capable of . . . I wanted to show them that . . .

My thoughts stopped there.

There was *nothing* to show them. Wasn't I making that absolutely clear?

Clear as a bell.

Each of these experiences was a cable that connected my self-confidence and courage to a lever I struggled not to press. The fortress my entire family had helped me construct, and that I had made my own, trembled in front of me, making me lose my balance until I fell on the detonator.

Everything got thrown into the air.

Luckily I'm good at building things. And I knew that, little by little, I would rebuild my fortress again, even if it took me a long time.

A SIESTA

A fter that visit to the doctor, I found myself wishing I wouldn't keep growing.

Growing had stopped me from riding a bike anymore.

Growing was giving me back problems.

And growing was precisely what my pectoral muscles didn't do.

Now it was up to me to get used to the idea. It would never happen, just like when I was little and had to get over my false hopes about my arm. I'd learned that the hard way, when my little sister, Naia, was born.

Her birth was also a day like any other. Needless to say, it was much less dramatic than my own. The flowers people gave my mother were much happier than the ones they gave her when I was born, and Naia emerged with two whole little arms. That was a deception, I won't deny it. Part of my four-year-old self hoped to create a team of superheroes with my sister, like Batman and Robin or Jessie and James, but triumphing in all their endeavors. We'd be the Super-abled, and no one could stop our tricks.

Around me everyone was very moved by Naia's arrival. Even at school, my teacher asked about my mother and my future little sister or brother, if I was happy, if I was looking forward to being a big brother, if I wanted my new sibling to be a boy or girl, what names I wanted the baby to be called . . . I answered quickly and almost cuttingly, as if I were ashamed. They encouraged me and told me having a little sibling was cool and that I'd always have someone to play with. I only half paid attention because I wasn't really interested, to tell the truth. I was more focused on another event that was about to happen and would be much cooler than the birth of my little sister: the growth of my arm.

Yes, I can confess this without even being ashamed. When I was four, I was completely and absolutely convinced my arm would finally grow. After watching a documentary about starfish one afternoon when my parents fell asleep on the sofa, I knew that the exact same thing had happened to me: I lost the arm (I must have left it behind in my mother's belly), and now I had to grow another one.

I thought I just needed to eat well in order to grow; no wonder old people always insisted so much that I eat fruit and finish my *acelgas*. And I hadn't even listened to them!

"Well, well, David," Mamá exclaimed, "it's nice to see you suddenly like your vegetables!"

"He doesn't want his little sister to take his place as the best child in the world," Papá said. "Right, kid?"

I didn't want to tell them they were wrong. I wanted to give them a surprise when my arm grew. It would take time, I knew that; after all, I had to compensate for all those years and years of not eating any vegetables at all. And luckily it would grow back after Naia was in our lives. This way we'd have time to be the Super-abled!

Everything was going to turn out great—I was sure of it. But how could I keep such a secret? I started to see progress and was afraid the growth would be so fast everyone would realize. At the same time, every day I was more and more excited. It was obvious in everything I did, but people thought it was because I was going to have a little sister. With Naia, I had the perfect excuse and the ideal alibi, so nobody realized the changes my body was going through. Everyone was worried about my mother (her belly, bigger every day) and about Naia (was she growing properly inside there?). My arm, for once in my life, didn't matter.

I don't need to tell you that it wasn't growing at all, right? I might lack something else, but I had no shortage of imagination.

After nine months the ordinary day arrived. Flowers at the hospital, congratulatory cards, and not a sign of any pamphlets of abusive and disrespectful orthopedists. Naia was born with two arms, two legs, and all her fingers and toes. She wasn't missing anything, nor did she have anything extra. There, beside her hospital bed, in my mother's room, I realized my little arm hadn't grown even a millimeter, and needless to say I also understood that my missing half an arm wasn't still inside my mother's belly, but instead . . .

"Naia took it."

"What's that, *cielo*?" my mother asked, half-asleep. She was worn out after so many visitors, and my *abuela* didn't stop asking her to rest a bit.

"Naia kept it," I muttered. Hadn't she heard me? It was obvious what I meant.

"Kept what?"

"My arm!" I shouted. "That arm is mine!"

I didn't pay much attention to the faces my *abuela* and parents must have made. I was too busy staring at Naia, that little sister who was so tiny and seemed so defenseless but who had stolen my arm. I'm sure they must have made a grimace of mixed tenderness and pity (what I call *"penura,"* mixing *pena* and *ternura*) and wondered how they were going to explain things to me. They did manage to explain it, and I understood. I didn't dwell on it too much, although despite clearly remembering my superhero fantasies and my starfish theories, I don't remember what exactly they told me. I guess, just as how something in my mind went *click* when I saw that starfish documentary, the same mechanism was activated again when I saw my sister for the first time.

The truth is very simple, much simpler than the regenerative mechanism of echinoderms: Naia had been born with two arms, and I hadn't.

And that was it. That truth wasn't going to suddenly grow, revealing new and mysterious pathways.

With twelve years behind my aching back, things hadn't changed. While Mamá searched for a solution so I could practice swimming without any problems, I locked myself in my room and barely left it. I built LEGOs and practiced guitar. By this time I already used Papá's portable computer to plan my constructions. Planes, above all. I also did my homework. I came out only to play video games in the living room, with the hope Papá might join me. But he didn't; he remained locked in his studio, playing at being a mechanic. We didn't know what he was doing, and my mother swore she hadn't the least idea, either, no matter how a little twisted smile escaped her.

"Ferran! Don't make me call you again!" she shouted one Saturday night. "Dinner is ready!"

So ready Naia and I had almost finished the first course. Papá was taking longer than usual to leave his studio. When he arrived at the table, he made a big announcement: "I've finished what I was making! Tomorrow I'll show it to you all."

I played with the last peas that remained on my plate without much emotion.

"Well, I've figured out how we can help David swim without feeling bad!" my mother exclaimed.

That didn't manage to cheer me up, either. I didn't have the strength to pretend I was happy. I was tired of not doing anything, sad because I felt like I was turning into an increasingly malformed giant. But I also didn't feel like spending every afternoon swimming, nor did I care about whatever gadget Papá had been building for the past month and a half.

"I've spoken to Carles's mother. It seems they have a heated pool at home, and they'll let us use it a few days a week. Did you hear that, David? After school you can go to Carles's house and be with him while you swim."

Great, now even my best friends pitied me. Why not create a charity devoted just to me? The whole town could donate to it!

"How cool! Can I go swimming, too? Pleeeeeeaaase." Of course Naia wasn't going to miss the chance for a swim.

"I didn't know Carles's family had a pool. Since when? Last time we went to their place for a barbecue, I didn't see it," Papá commented.

"It seems they installed it last summer. She explained everything when I told her about our situation. They built it over the winter, because it's cheaper then, and . . ."

"Why don't we do the same thing?" my father asked her.

"Are you crazy? That's something rich people do, and we can't afford it."

Stubborn, Papá insisted. "Look, Nathalie, I'm going to speak to the developer who's going to build our house on the plot, and instead of three floors, I'm going to suggest he make it only two and that he calculate how much it would cost to put in a heated pool next to the garage instead. With all the machinery and everything included, that way we don't exceed the initial budget."

All this just to make my life easier and help me, as they've always done.

It didn't take much to convince my mother to go along with Papá's sudden mad idea.

"So you see, we're going to sell the apartment, and we'll finally make our plan to build a house on the empty lot a reality," my mother explained. "What do you think about having your own pool, David?"

"Mine too!" Naia said, making us all laugh.

"And yours, too, Naia, yours, too, of course."

I didn't know which way to cast my thoughts: toward the future pool or toward my father's surprise. Did whatever he'd been building in secret have something to do with me? For the rest of dinner I was nervous, imagining what it might be. Sometimes, my father can be very . . . extra, though not extra in the sense of a bit part in a movie but in the sense of extraordinary. He can turn any tiny thing into a spectacle, whether writing a song he plays and sings with his band like some superstar at the local festival or putting together a gymkhana, a field day of competitions to show off horsemanship. Sometimes it can be overwhelming, like just then: thinking maybe he'd built me a gigantic exoskeleton to defeat my enemies and save the world from an invasion of evil angels. These thoughts worried me so much I could hardly swallow dessert. But in general, Papá's songs and his mad ideas brought joy into our lives and could turn an insignificant moment into something unforgettable.

After all, he had always been my guide in our games of *rompecuellos*, had bought me my first chocolate egg with the little toy inside, and had given me, together with my mother, my first LEGO set to improve and develop my abilities. He also taught me how to ride a bike.

"When you're finished with breakfast, come to the garage, OK?" he told me the next day.

I was about to sink my teeth into my pancakes. Mamá makes them on Sundays whenever Naia or I am sad. Thanks to me, we'd gotten pancakes four Sundays in a row. Something good had to come out of thinking your body was avenging itself on you, right? Although I don't know who was happier: me eating pancakes or my mother making them for us.

Normally those pancakes tasted like heaven. They had to be made of whatever my broken dreams were made of, because otherwise I can't explain it. But when Papá came and said that to me, they turned into sand, the syrup was like cement, and the whipped cream tasted bitter. Even so, I kept eating. My father's surprise wouldn't quench my stomach's noises, and I was afraid to go and find the exoskeleton he had prepared for me, so I tried to draw out breakfast for so long I didn't even care when Naia wanted to throw cream on me for fun.

When Mamá yelled at my sister for getting syrup all over the table and there wasn't even a speck left on my own plate, I finally went out to the garage. Along the way, my bike greeted me, as bitter and dusty as ever, but this time I felt it had a sadness, as if it were also frightened by what might happen. And you better believe that if I'd known what was waiting inside for me, I would have understood my old bike's sadness. Yes, I would have gotten just as nervous, but I assure you it wouldn't have been for the same reasons.

When I pushed open the door, I found my father squatting down, cleaning a grown-up bicycle. That bicycle, however, had something unique that no other bike had, not grown-up ones, not kiddie bikes—and no, I'm not talking about alloy wheels or front-wheel drive. From the right side of the handlebar protruded something that looked kind of like a plunger. In reality it was a small iron bar he'd soldered to the handlebar with the help of his faithful friend Manolo Conteras. The bar ended in a sort of prosthesis made from black leather, concave like a small chalice.

Papá turned around and gave me a big smile.

"Do you like it?"

"What . . . What is it?"

"Why, it's a bicycle, David. What else would it be?" He didn't stop smiling at my shock, because even though I was acting like a fool, I really couldn't believe what was happening.

"I can see that, but what's that . . . stick?"

"Come on, come closer."

My hands trembled with emotion, and my legs almost gave way. Could that be . . . ? I rested my fingers on the handlebar extension.

"Get on, you'll see." I did as he indicated. "Now you just need to rest your little arm on the leather tip. Like that. Does it fit OK? It's lined with a material that won't rub and won't get hot. You'll see."

Yes, it was what I had suspected the moment I opened the door: a grown-up bicycle made especially to fit me. No matter how many words I could use over a thousand hours, I couldn't come close to describing how I felt just then.

Unsure, I mounted the bike and proved it was adapted perfectly to my body. That wall that was so tall, so strong, so unbreakable into which I had been determined to turn my anatomy crumbled before my eyes thanks to my father's inventiveness. The fact that I had never wanted to wear a prosthetic for myself didn't mean the bicycle couldn't have one. But above all the fact that bicycles were adapted to only normative bodies shouldn't mean all other anatomies couldn't ride one.

Immediately we left the garage, my father trotting after me as I pedaled away as if it hadn't been more than a year since I'd ridden a bike. The problem with my earlier bike wasn't just that I had to lean over too far and to one side in order to rest my *bracito* against the handlebar but that the bike had gotten too small for me in general; my legs were too bent once my feet touched the ground, and my butt didn't even fit on the seat anymore.

"I realized right away your old bike wasn't any good for you anymore, even if you had two arms," my father explained. "But I didn't know how to resolve the issue of the handlebar."

I rode circles around him. He couldn't stop laughing, and I was in the clouds. Perhaps I could even fly with my new bike. The wind caressed my face, and my knees started to feel stiff after so long without giving them a workout like this. I could stand up from the seat and keep pedaling. I had a wide range of movement.

"So I was thinking about it for months. How could you lean against the handlebar? What was missing for you?"

As he spoke, he approached the garage and grabbed his own bicycle. Every member of the family had one, and some weekends we went out for a ride, all four of us together. That was what I had missed most during that past year.

We decided to give my old bike to the son of Manolo, my father's dear friend who he always turned to when he needed a favor and who I always think of as an example of true friendship. The look of happiness on his son Manel's face was indescribable.

We pedaled away from home. Papá had to ask me a few times to not go so fast and had to pick up the pace to keep up with me. I couldn't stop pedaling and pedaling. I wanted to ride circles around the entire city. I wanted the whole world to see me. I wanted to pedal all day and all night. I wanted to ride around the whole world.

"You couldn't reach the handlebar," Papá continued explaining during our ride, "so I told myself: if David can't reach the handlebar, the handlebar will have to reach David. That was something that could be fixed, right? So I spoke to all the bicycle manufacturers, David. I assure you. I explained the situation to them and told them what was missing. But it was completely devastating. It was one 'no' after another. All the companies, with their engineers, said there was nothing that could be done! That it was impossible! So I decided I'd have to take care of it by myself. To design it and build it. And here we are."

There was no shame in saying it felt just then that I didn't have arms enough to embrace him with love and appreciation for what he had done.

"Don't thank me. It could be much better. And one day it'll be too small for you; you're growing every day. We feed you too well." He laughed. "When that happens, we'll have to make adjustments. Perhaps we'll need to change the materials, make it with a longer bar. We'll see. Although maybe next time you could give us a hand . . ."

Yes, Papá was right. Despite the wall having crumbled, reality still was what it was, and the condition of my body was unchangeable. My arm might not grow, but I did—more than ever during the years to come. I outgrew that bike, or better yet, that prosthetic, and we needed another to avoid more back pain and another painful revelation.

"We'll play it as it goes," I told him. "We'll leave that victory for another day, for when the next battle comes."

My father nodded and agreed with me, with a proud smile on his lips. That morning helped me understand many things. Especially how much I loved my father and the importance of never lowering my guard in the face of adversity. It would have been hard to know which of us was happier: he for having been able to help me or me for finding joy once more in the little everyday things of life.

Of course, my parents weren't the only ones who were always by my side. A few weeks after I started to ride the new bike, I crashed—monumentally. How big a wipeout? you ask. In a contest of falls, I wouldn't have won first place because they'd have just named me the indisputable world champion of blowouts and canceled the competition.

My sister and I were taking a ride along a path on the outskirts of our neighborhood when I wanted to get too far ahead of her as a way of annoying Naia and wound up sinking into a treacherous hole someone must have dug. I went flying even higher than when Papá gave me the bike and I thought I was floating with happiness.

Oh, the pain! It wasn't anything serious. I didn't break or twist anything, but even now I still can't understand it. How could I have given myself just a handful of bruises (really big ones, it's true) and a few scratches if the fall was so colossal that my sister squealed and came running to help me? As if she were one of the doctors on the series we watched on TV, she looked me over from head to toe to check if I had any wounds. Naia and I had always been a team, even if her mere birth ruined my plans to form the Squad of the Super-abled. On one occasion, I don't remember when or why, I heard her tell my mother, "I don't want my arm, Mami. I want to be like David, who's really cool."

"And what shall we do with the extra arm?" Mamá asked her, playing along.

"Well, we can give it away to someone. If David doesn't need it, I don't, either. The two of us, to the ends of the world . . ."

My sister is always willing to help me. And I her. That afternoon I banged myself up good, and it was hard for me to get up, but not just because of the aches and pain. I also had the sensation that, if I'd had two hands, I might have been able to grab the handlebar better, control the spin, and the fall might have been less severe. I was scared I'd never stop injuring myself in life, that I'd keep hitting obstacles—obstacles I might overcome, yes, but with pain and effort.

Remember what I said earlier? If you fall, you nurse your wounds, then get up and try again. But at that moment it was an effort to get up. I was tired, and it took me a while longer to understand that being tired isn't bad.

Sometimes what you need is to rest. To lie there after the fall, give time for the pain to settle, and wait. Alongside your family, who surround you and support you all the time. They are the best medicine, the balm that, used properly, with patience and lots of affection, can help you to endure the impasse and the rest.

That's what I did when I was a teenager.

But don't get too comfortable.

Because you have to get up later.

There's no option for not doing so.

Naia remained with me until I stopped hurting from the fall. Then we got up and went home.

Together. To the end of the world and beyond.

EXPLOSIONS

I t's hard to rest when everything around you is flying through the air.

Whenever something in my life was resolved, a new difficulty appeared. Sometimes, and depending on my mood, that could even be amusing, like an obstacle course. David Aguilar, Olympic champion in hurdling. Other times it could be worse than a field of land mines, and who can rest like that?

For the moment I concentrated on swimming and my recovered passion for cycling. Really, I couldn't thank my father enough for what he'd done with the bicycle. I was obsessed with my superbike (that's what I'd called it). The sensation it caused when I went out on rides was overwhelming. Everyone stared at me, fascinated, and made me feel special, but positively this time. My physical difference was transformed into a superpower that, together with my sister's support, made me feel like someone unique. Now, the *rompecuellos* had done a 180; my passage no longer seemed to generate pity but admiration. With my three-handlebarred superbike, I left people awed in my wake, and my attitude changed: I felt like I could change the world, help break and destroy the stigma of disability. Because we're not disabled, just differently abled. *Diff-abled.*

In short, with the superbike I became just another cyclist—overprotected, that was true, but just one more in the crowd. One who enjoyed his rides and putting on speed, the breeze on his legs, the smell of the pines in the forests that circled the city.

Nonetheless, it wasn't long before I faced the first hurdle. It's not easy performing acrobatics on a bicycle and even less so with only one hand. Papá would need to invent a new extension for me to make jumps or do a wheelie. This time I'd help him; I was getting better and better with my LEGO constructions, which I started to mix with Bionicle sets (the humanoid LEGO toy characters that had stories behind them) to make real advances: cranes, drawbridges with their own mechanism, even little cars I wound up myself. I reused equipment from here and there, little devices I'd played with when I was a squirt and that I gave a second life to now. If I had learned something, it's that nothing that was created for one use was useful only for that single thing, and I considered myself to be living proof of that maxim. Sometimes things don't turn out as you expect, and in order to resolve it, you've got to play the cards life has dealt you. Remember that an ace can be the lowest card in the deck but also the highest.

Thinking like this, I might become a card dealer in a casino. Or even better, perhaps I could study engineering. It'd be good to help people somehow, with little pieces, jacks, and mechanisms that could make their life easier, no?

The thing is, a hurdle appeared before me, and I almost crashed into it instead of going over it. Luckily it was an obstacle we already knew very well: growth spurts. Of course—and even if I sometimes wished for the opposite to happen—I continued growing and stretching out. I got taller and taller with every day. That was something that, on the one hand, was a relief. I wouldn't be short! But on the other, it worried me. As we've seen, I would once more outgrow my bike.

The moment came to confront that battle.

Fortunately I'd been resting.

Now, a few years after the first modification, I was in perfect shape to confront this battle.

"We need something longer," I commented to my father.

It was obvious.

"Yes, I've been thinking. Some material that's even lighter than the steel."

"Exactly."

He stood there thinking for a while and suddenly remembered a good childhood friend who'd been a big kayaker and now devoted himself to repairing these really expensive carbon fiber canoes and oars, a material used today in various kinds of canoe craft. Without hesitating even a second, Papá grabbed his phone and called his friend, with a smile on his face.

"Sergi, do you think you could help us? It's about David. I have to adapt the prosthetic I made for his bike, and I thought of you and all you know about carbon."

"Ferran, my friend! Of course I will. I'm in Parc del Segre. I'll wait for you here this very afternoon. For David, anything you need."

I overheard them and was taken by surprise. It was incredible how everyone pitched in to help my dad and me succeed day after day.

My father had great lifelong friends from his *pueblo*, Seu d'Urgell. Since we needed to adapt not only the prosthetic but also the brake system (you hadn't thought of that, had you?), he had in mind to call on a few more friends who would surely lend us a hand.

After calling Sergi, Papá visited Joan and Jordi at their workshop and gave them a design for a homemade system of brakes that would require their skills to create. My father explained the system and its functioning, so I could activate both brakes with a single handlebar.

They managed to fabricate it in less than an hour, and when my father pulled out his wallet to pay them, they quickly dismissed him. It wasn't a question of money; they'd done it only to help. To make me happy with a useful prosthetic.

That afternoon we went to Sergi's workshop. He was waiting for us with a big smile, thrilled to be able to help us with this project we were so excited about. When he saw us come in with the superbike, he abandoned what he was doing and focused all his attention on us. My father explained his ideas for adapting the bike for me again, but this time using the material for which Sergi was widely known: carbon fiber.

With a gesture Sergi indicated we should follow him through a door behind the counter that always remained ajar. Behind it was a larger space than I had guessed, with tall metal shelves that were full of neatly ordered pieces, replacements, and gadgets of all kinds. While my father explained to him in astonishing detail how we'd thought the new and improved extension of the handlebar should be, Sergi, who was paying close attention to everything Papá said, went from one shelf to another, climbed up a ladder with wheels, slid along on it, congratulated us for our ideas, or recommended we do this or that.

He dumped different pieces on one of the worktables: extendible springs, flexible rods, rubber, tires, screws, nuts, cogs, keys . . . Everything we might need could be found there.

"Look," he told us, motioning at the collection of objects arrayed on the table. "With all this I think we can make something that might work."

Papá, who was behind me, contemplating all the stuff, shook my shoulder.

They took my measurements, and we agreed to come back the following week to try the new extension for the superbike.

But since we were so anxious to see the evolution of my contraption, Sergi sent us some photos, which Papá immediately posted on his Facebook page and which generated a significant current of chatter. From that moment on, my father's social media had tremendous success, as he posted everything related to my achievements.

I nervously waited for the weekend. I was eager to ride my bike on another level. With my professional helmet, my leggings . . . A higher level!

"So what do you have for us, Sergi? We're dying to see it," my father said as we entered the workshop the following Saturday.

Sergi pulled out his adaptation fabricated from carbon and left us speechless. He'd used some flan molds for my little hand to fit into and a PVC tube lined with carbon that was affixed to the handlebar by inserting it into the extreme of the right side.

"You're going to be able to ride like never before, David," my father stated.

I don't remember the exact timing, but in the end it took Sergi maybe a little more than a week to build the new extension. Every time they thought it was finished and we tried it on one of the workshop bikes, we realized it was missing some bit. It seemed like the never-ending story—the never-ridden bike. We might have given up, but we couldn't just shrug our shoulders and move on to something else. Each new error was a new challenge that, no matter how disheartened we were by the setback, pushed us to keep trying to overcome it. When something failed, didn't fit, or simply fell apart, I smiled, because that meant we were closer to the goal.

And we would cross it, all three of us together.

In the test of (what we didn't know would be) the final version of the prosthesis, all the final adjustments had helped tremendously in resolving the problems we'd found. At last the extension was perfect for me.

"Sergi, tell me what we owe you for the prosthetic," my father said. "David wants to try it as soon as possible."

He pulled out his wallet, but his friend made my father put it away.

"Nothing, Ferran. Forget about that for now."

We didn't know how to respond.

Placing his hand on my father's shoulder, Sergi whispered that what he, my father, was doing for me, his son, was a great example. And he added, "I'm delighted to help you. All of us here are happy to help you." He spread his arms, indicating the warehouse, the workshop, the town. "Your son deserves to be able to ride a bicycle and do anything else he wants to do. All the boys like him deserve that. If only more of them had a father like you."

I couldn't feel prouder of my family and our friends.

Whenever I rode my superbike, I remembered how I'd gotten it, and I also recalled that first bike I'd learned to ride on, the one we bought from Joan Erola, an old friend of my father who would turn into an indispensable guide for me. Joan had led me through the aisles of the store, showing me all the bicycles for kids: blue, red, green, fuchsia, turquoise, red, lavender . . . There were bikes in so many colors I'm sure rainbows were jealous. With my father following behind us and without giving any sign of noticing my *bracito*, Joan encouraged me to pick the bike I liked the most.

"It's a very special moment, so take your time. We'll look at the entire store if need be."

The store was a business between friends, but that didn't mean it was small. They were former champions of skiing and kayaking, sports that are very popular in the region and had produced great champions, like them. A bicycle store for sportspeople with dreams, where their efforts as former glories of the past are an inspiration for the young, myself included. A store created with a lot of effort and sacrifice, my father explained to me, proud of his friends.

Speaking of friends, whenever I rode the bike, I showed off with my mates. Everyone stared at me in shock and awe, and some even stopped me to check out that unique contraption: the antenna that connected my arm to the bike and managed to transport me wherever I wanted to go. I was attuned to the bicycle and to the world, more and more every day.

I've never again felt like I did during those first weeks I rode it. I got used to that "glove" feel right away, and soon it lost the magic. But it truly was magical! The glove feel was just that: I could feel on my very skin how that bicycle fit me perfectly, just like a glove.

When Papá gave me the first bike with the prosthetics, adaptation to my world became *cap per avall*, as we say here in Andorra, or upside down; it was like moving from plane X to plane Y. But with an extension as ergonomic as this new one, the sensation was very different. Everything was even more perfect, like discovering an entirely new plane of existence, a z-axis that changed everything. I felt like a derivative stretching into infinity. Limits didn't exist.

As you grow up—or rather, as you climb up a very long, steep, rocky hill your entire life—you realize that the most precious moments are so because they don't last. Although they pass, and although they're no longer here because they've blown away, you've lived them, and the beautiful memories of that joy remain forever scattered throughout your body.

Unfortunately the detonators that surrounded my life were connected and ready to carry out their mission. And I knew, despite not being wholly aware of it, the bike could stumble against any pebble on the path, go flying, and fall on a detonator, making the explosive go off.

◆ ◆ ◆

But that moment would come later.

What didn't have any delay in arriving was, of course, the problem. It came in the shape of my classmate Jordi, as was already becoming a habit. Then I swallowed every dip in the road and made the leap over the hundred trucks, but I faltered over the thirtieth and landed on the thirty-seventh. Well, no; there was no landing. I crashed—pretty hard. One of the real blowouts of my life.

One day I'll make a top-ten list of the wildest thrashings I've given myself, both figuratively and literally. Position four would go to the fall I took when I was fourteen because of Jordi. Unfortunately I'm speaking of a literal fall, a real, physical fall. With pain in every nerve ending, everywhere: skin, muscles, and bones.

Bodies are really important, and I think most people don't understand that or don't assume it or don't see it clearly; they think the world is a certain way and that's that. I, of course, with one fewer arm (according to some), realized it right away. Well, not so fast. I was five when I had my first collision with reality. But that's a story for another time.

For now I'll tell you about how people see their own bodies. For a time I think people see themselves as equal to everyone else because of having the adequate number of extremities and fingers and cartilage, like kids doing roll call during an outing: Are my two arms there? I didn't lose a leg along the way? Oh, I've left a finger at home! But little by little, they notice more differences: this one has a larger body than I do, or a shorter one, or a broader one, or their head has the shape of . . . And then there comes the shorty, the fatty, the bigheaded dude, the guy with big hands, the *manco* . . . But really we're all exactly alike. We are all simply a compilation of pieces joined together by some form of magic. My category of *manco* is part of the same compilation of bodies; it's just mine usually got extra disapproval points for being less common than being a "ball of lard" or a "melon head."

And that was exactly what one of Jordi's minions said to my pal Enric: "Hey, you, lardball!"

That set off my warning antenna, because I wasn't going to let someone treat my friend like that. Enric had put on weight that summer. His body was no longer the same as always. It had suddenly changed, and now he was seen as different. Although he didn't have as many oddness points as me (nobody was going to beat me at that at my school), being fat was definitely enough for someone to give you grief.

Quickly I put myself between the two of them.

"What are you going to do? You don't even have a hand to punch me with!" he mocked me.

"Let me remind you I'm a leftie."

"Ooh, I'm so scared!" The kid laughed, looking to Jordi and the others, pointing at me, making fun of me.

It was always like this; it had been like this for ages, and I almost didn't care. I'd lowered my head and stuck the end of my sleeve in the pocket of my pants. But that wasn't enough for them. They also tried to take away my joy in riding a bike, playing a sport, moving freely . . . They had devoted themselves to making my life impossible.

But there was something they didn't know: they weren't going to take away the joy of being with my friends. They could throw everything they wanted at me, but I wasn't going to let them mess with my friends. With the tailored clothes my mother made for me, I had managed to feel like a superhero for a time, and although that time had been brief, it had left me with a strong sense of justice.

And at fourteen, justice came down to a very clear maxim: mess with my friends, and you'll pay the price.

Without thinking twice, I got up in the kid's face, although I had no idea what I was going to do. Was I going to hit him? Was I really that kind of person? My friends took a step forward to stop me or help me—I never managed to find out. Before even deciding for myself what I intended to do with my unexpected bravery, I was already stretched out on the ground.

I fell on my butt.

Literally.

The fall was so hard I felt each of my vertebrae clack against the next, provoking a deafening vibration that spread throughout my entire body, from my feet to the *muñón*, and stuffed my ears.

". . . vid! . . . vid!"

". . . to! What . . . say?"

". . . uel! . . . di! . . . lot . . . tor!"

That was all I heard.

My friends and a teacher helped me get up. Meanwhile, other teachers were reading the riot act to those creeps. Or at least that's what I imagined. Everything was moving around me, quick movements I, however, saw in slow motion, as if two velocities coincided in time and space, not in a parallel fashion but unified. It was as if I were watching an episode of *Doctor Who*.

What a trip.

I could get up without too much problem but with a horrible pain in my rear—one of those you know will only get worse and worse over the course of the day. While the teaching staff worried if I'd lost any mobility and argued about whether to call an ambulance, the only thing I wondered was how long before I could get to the nurse and beg for an entire box of painkillers. I couldn't quite understand why they were so worried. It was only later that I learned my impact had been heard throughout the schoolyard, and those who had seen the push Jordi had given me were shocked by his brutality. Go figure. I, who had lived through it, thought they were exaggerating and could remember only the fall itself.

What I think affected me more was not the physical fall but the one my emotions took, which got more intense over the rest of the day, just like the pain right where the back loses its chaste name. It's incredible how, in just seconds, we can go from joy that borders on euphoria to the deepest sadness, the most animal-like rage, the sharpest and most wounding frustration.

That morning, like on so many others, I'd gone to school with my mother. I thought it would be an ordinary day, without incidents. My math exam on quadratic equations would go well; I had studied a lot.

That afternoon, much earlier than scheduled, I left school in my mother's car instead of walking to her travel agency. The pain in my butt hadn't stopped increasing, and when it reached the point where I didn't know how to sit at my desk any longer, I told the teacher, and they called home. We went to the emergency room, fearing the crash might have damaged my coccyx. In the end maybe no one had been exaggerating.

I was the one who had distorted reality, because I couldn't believe it was really happening.

Would it always be like this?

That, as you already know, wasn't the first time.

Nor was it the last.

BRUISES
AND GETTING
KNOCKED SILLY

I don't want to *go out with you*. You're missing an arm and . . ."

You already know those words and how they made me feel. It wasn't just disappointment, nor did I simply feel sad. It was much more.

It's curious how pain works. When Jordi pushed me, the anguish and frustration it caused me were worse than the crash, whereas Marta's messages, more than wounding my feelings, had made me waste away physically.

Her excuses were like a beating with words. Right away I started to feel like I couldn't get enough air, as if I'd been punched in the stomach, or like when you belly flop into the pool and start swallowing water from the shock. That's how it was for me when I threw myself into Marta's pool. It wasn't an empty pool (which I would have preferred) but one full of answers, agony, and disdain that I swallowed until my lungs were filled and I couldn't breathe. Even today I'm amazed I was able to archive the chat without blocking her and that I didn't throw my phone as far as possible so it broke into a gazillion pieces.

I couldn't breathe, my chest hurt, and my head reverberated, but her messages wouldn't stop flashing in my mind like cell phone notifications. I wanted only to get home and slam the door. That wasn't physical; there was no wound or bruise or anything that could make my nerve endings quiver like that. However, I hurt as if there was one, and I became aware of all the parts of my body. Even my right forearm.

Pain works like that. It seems to join body and mind, sinking its talons deep into the flesh and causing spasms that create mysterious connections. Thus, an accident numbs your senses, and words block your breathing.

That time when I fell on my coccyx was nothing. Luckily.

At least for me. The aches lasted a few weeks, it's true, but I was able to go about my life like normal. Jordi and his goons, on the other hand, didn't have the same luck. They were suspended from school for a week. Each of them had a disciplinary mark in their record, and I was greeted with applause from my classmates when I returned to school the next day. For a few days I became the class hero without knowing quite why. I think my entire body still vibrated from the fall, like some sort of tuning fork.

The only thing I was missing was to have broken my coccyx; I imagined I'd rattle like maracas whenever I walked or ran, or maybe jangle like when you've got a bunch of coins in your pants pocket.

It took me a few days to get back to normal. The vibrations were really caused by the shock I got after the fall. In fact, when I went to the hospital, the nurse who attended me when I arrived insisted on that more than on the fall itself. Sometimes, he explained to us, the shock can prove worse than the wound itself; it might hide the pain of internal bleeding or make me lose my appetite for a few days. The doctor who visited me later, unlike the nurse, thought it was because of my arm.

The only thing that kept me calm in those days was the swimming I did for my back and chest. We now had our own pool at home and didn't need to depend on Carles and his family. I no longer got to enjoy the bountiful *meriendas* his mother prepared for us as a snack—not to mention Carles's help with my Catalan homework—but at least I once more had my own space and my privacy. Papá designed an annex to the building right next to the garage so the pool was covered, and he installed some showers and a heater so it could be used all year long. Thus, I had an entertainment area all for myself, available every day of the year, for when I was in the mood or when I should practice, and I no longer had to depend on the kindness of my friends two days a week.

"Carles, don't you care that I always go to your house to swim?" I'd asked him one day as we ate our *meriendas* together, after I'd done my obligatory exercises. Then it would be time for us to do homework, and my father would come and get me once he was done working for the day.

My friend stared at me without quite understanding and asked me why it should bother him for me to come to his house and use his pool. His mother, he assured me, was delighted to be able to help us in some way, and with me around he wasn't so bored doing his homework. I, however, was going through a time of insecurity that didn't let me think with even the least amount of logic.

"Because of my half arm." He still didn't understand. "Doesn't it disgust you?"

He looked at me in complete silence during what felt like five or even ten minutes, although it wasn't more than a few seconds, then answered, "Man, we've been friends since preschool. What do you think?"

Although it was a rhetorical question, I couldn't answer him. I didn't dare to do so, not even if I was able to finish formulating the thought in my head.

"What disgusts me is that you think you're disgusting. You're not strange, you're unique. And that's very special."

It's no secret that I had, and sometimes still have, my bad moments—days, weeks, or even months in which I believe I'm really disabled. Luckily I had my friends and family to keep me moving forward and continuing to succeed. I leaned on them as if they were a crutch, and that helped me get up and take flight once more.

They are my prosthesis.

The only prosthesis I need.

I admit that at first my father's plan to build a heated pool at home was a bit of a bore to me. It meant the construction would take even longer, with more dust, more noise . . . I wanted only to rest a bit, to wallow in my own sadness until I could get up once more. But soon after I started riding the first superbike, and it gave me back my strength and helped me feel more enthusiastic about the pool project. With my energy restored, I discovered the joy of swimming, which until then was just an activity I performed as an obligation. I hated it because it reminded me, day after day, of my lacks, my anatomical absences, everything people insisted on pointing out to me to call me "different." Something I also did back then.

Have you ever had the feeling of belonging? Of feeling you're in the right place at the right moment? Of floating on air, despite being aware your feet are on the ground or you're paddling in the water? That's how I felt when swimming, stroke after stroke, with my clever modified hand mitt. Papá invented a mechanism that held my waist with a belt, which, tied with a climbing cord to the parquet, kept me straight while I swam. With this device I didn't move forward, do laps, or swim from one side of the pool to the other, but I didn't need to, either. I swam to train the muscles of my arms, back, and chest, and with the arm strokes, I managed to train them more than enough, even if I stayed in place. It was like being on a treadmill but in the water, breathing through a snorkel and moving my entire body.

With this practice, the aches went away much faster. The therapy worked, and I liked swimming more and more every day. Each breath was like a hinge that kept the arm strokes joined together in each piece of that puzzle called the body. I felt my muscles work with precision and in detail, like a machine that was now well oiled. I loved being in the water. That's how the vibrations after the fall disappeared in under a few weeks.

For a few years, I followed my pool exercises strictly and also tried to go out on my bike on weekends. I helped my dad and Sergi with adapting the prostheses from time to time. When you add in my LEGO constructions, these activities calmed me down and took up all my free time.

Yes, those small square plastic pieces still filled my life, and I didn't tire of them. Especially not since I'd built the first prosthesis when I was nine, helped by a shoelace, some Bionicle robots that I began to experiment with dismantling, some adhesive tape, and the classic LEGO bricks. That was how I started with the Bionicles. With them I felt like a mad scientist creating his small army of little monsters; I was the powerful Frankenstein but less crazy and without a horde of townspeople wanting to attack my creations. Unlike him, I had more ingenuity and wasn't playing at creating life; I was just obsessed with anthropomorphic figures. For me they were toy soldiers, really powerful ones, whose anatomic complexity both challenged and intrigued me. Do you remember them? They had fantastic proportions that seemed, at least to me, to be a hybrid of animal and human. Some had large arched feet like those of a dinosaur, and others even had wings or enormous claws on their hands and feet.

The bodies resembled humans but were different in the end. They were very cool. I wasn't the only one obsessed with them. At the LEGO store, other kids bought them, and many begged their parents to give them to them as gifts.

They were almost robotic humans, metallic, with bodies that diverged from the norm—kinda like me (but with more metal).

It made me think: If we really were missing an eleventh finger, what if we were also missing wings, a tail, or claws? Maybe we lack these things, but even so, we've managed to adapt. We've invented planes to fly, learned to live without an appendix, adapted to the world with what life's given us. I'm missing an arm; Peggy is, too. Albert Llovera, former alpine skier from Andorra who was paralyzed in an accident, managed to do fancy tricks with his wheelchair and rally car. Many other people, all around the world, are in the same situation of *diff-ability*, and we can live pretty normally so long as the parking spots for people with *diff-abilities* aren't used by people who don't need them and things like that. (Although that's not my case, since my "disability" doesn't affect my mobility.)

Couldn't I really be extraordinary, special, like Carles told me? Could we all be? But not in the sense people usually think. I'm not talking about being *less*, or not managing it, or needing help from others but being *extra*ordinary. Learning to live outside the norms, with our own rules.

Challenging the everyday and overcoming it by using our brains.

Like when I tried to put together those Bionicles.

For me the best of all wasn't the challenge the figures entailed but being able to use their metallic and elastic pieces separately and melding them with my other LEGOs. Thus, I created an infinite number of things, like planes, bicycles, or helicopters, and I didn't need to fuss with the brackets, clips, and other materials found in the toolboxes my dad had at home or in his office.

Of course, there were also constructions whose pieces came all in a box, neatly ordered, which were just waiting for you in the store to be put together. But I wanted to go beyond that. I wanted to create from scratch and without instructions, using my instinct and experience in building things. Going beyond my limits relaxed me and gave me a sense of freedom I didn't get from swimming.

After all, I swam tied to the edge of the pool, until one day . . .

"Gah!"

I swallowed a lot of water by squealing like that, but I had really hurt myself. I still don't know how I managed to bang my foot in that way against one of the side walls. Maybe I miscalculated the distance from the middle of the pool when I started the exercise, or who knows what happened.

Angry at myself, I approached the edge, unfastened the belt, and emerged from the pool. It seemed like I hadn't done any damage. I could walk fine, and the only thing that hurt was my instep. It was red, and getting darker by the minute. I'd have a bruise. An enormous dark stain.

Ironically in biology class that week we'd gone over the circulatory system in depth, from arteries to capillaries. A bruise happened when the blow created a rupture in the capillaries of the area that was hit. Looking at the reddish skin, I could see beyond it and observe the blood spilling from the small broken veins to create the hematoma.

Without thinking twice, I got back in the water, and this time I concentrated much more on remaining in the center of the pool, which was just three meters wide and seven meters long.

However, I couldn't stop thinking about the future bruise I'd have and how such a silly misstep could lead to multiple breaks whose consequences expanded without anything stopping them until they wished to stop of their own volition.

That day was shortly after I had turned sixteen, maybe just a few weeks, and it was also right after my last fight. One event after the other setting off a graceful series of reactions.

It was during our snow excursion. We all were really eager to go skiing. It wouldn't be the typical school trip; there were no tiresome educational purposes that made the classes more unbearable. How many times did they take us on trips and make us do absurd homework afterward? They didn't just want us to listen to the museum guide of the day but also to retain every word we were told. Utter pointlessness.

But not this time; this was going to be a purely recreational excursion, the kind you thank your lucky stars for because of how rare they are.

We went skiing, and we were all psyched. Some bragged and said they would climb the black diamond slopes, and others fooled around with the idea of trying to snowboard. I was between both sides: I had gone to enjoy the snow and wasn't going to let anything or anyone get in the way of my plans, but I wasn't so crazy as to attempt the suicide slopes and defy the teachers. My new goal was to finish my ESO without another black mark on my record. In four years I'd already gotten into enough trouble. This trip was for us to have a good time and enjoy a day of exercise and fun.

The white slopes of the mountain shone intensely under the sun, blinding those of us who weren't wearing sunglasses or goggles. Mine were on the front table, and my mother's words reminding me not to forget them echoed in my mind along with the buzzing of the skiers who slid full speed down the slopes. After leaving our backpacks in the lodge, we collected our skis and hurried to take our turns going up the mountain on the cable car. The teachers asked us to be responsible as they sat us in pairs and reminded us we had to be back in the lodge by midday at the agreed-on time. We would all eat there before returning to school on the bus. We had all morning ahead of us to ski, organize innocent snowball fights, try snowboarding, and, of course, come back to the lodge for a hot chocolate.

After going up and down the slopes a few times, my friends and I decided to get some snowboards and try our luck. At worst we'd fall on our butts as we tried to challenge the laws of aerodynamics and gravity. We thought we'd stay on the first slope to break only the sound barrier (and not two or three of our bones), but once we got off the cable car, we kept climbing on foot a little more to make everything more interesting. That's what we were doing when Enric's foot went through the snow and he fell flat on the ground. He lifted his head up right away, and seeing his face covered in snow, we started to crack up.

"Thanks for asking if I'm OK!" he said after spitting out the snow as he tried to get up in fits and starts, sinking through the snow again and winding up on the ground with every step. Our stomachs started to ache from laughing so hard, and Enric began to throw snowballs at us as if he were a tennis ball machine. At first he missed with every throw, but when one hit me right in the face, I knew things were getting serious. What at first was a rout had turned into an attack. Álex and I knelt down and started to stockpile snowballs so we could throw them without having to stop. However, Enric wasn't an easy enemy to defeat. Not only was he quick in launching his own munitions, but also he was really agile and eluded all the snowballs we threw at him. He was so good at eluding them that, in the end, one of them wound up hitting someone who wasn't in our little group and who was heading toward one of the dangerous black diamond slopes. When he shook the snow off his head and I saw his face, my blood nearly froze.

"So you want a fight?" Jordi asked us defiantly. Without saying anything more, Marc, who was at his side, bent down quickly and threw a good handful of snow at us.

Enric, who was closer to them than to us, got hit in the eye, and I, of course, ran to defend him, throwing as many snowballs as I could with only one arm.

As was only logical and natural, it wasn't long before they came after me.

Now I think: Was that really necessary? Back then I still believed everything happened for a reason, that every act had its consequences, but there was no explanation according to that law for all the animosity and disgust those punks had for me. So did it give them a thrill to make fun of someone because of their physique, their way of dressing, or how they acted with other kids—and with me they just had a plus because I didn't have an arm? Did my *diff-ability* add points?

"You can't make even a single hit, *manco!*" Jordi humiliated me in front of everyone. Now it was not just my own friends who were witnessing the fight but also the rest of our classmates who were going up or down the slopes and had decided to stop to see for themselves how serious the situation was. For some, ending a field trip with a clean fistfight was the best thing that could happen. It would turn out to be a day of fun, rest, and spectacle.

But that wasn't going to happen.

"Hey," I replied, my hand full of snow, about to do something crazy if they didn't turn around and say they were sorry. "It's not my fault I'm missing an arm, OK?"

Marc smiled. It was a big smile, one that could have won first place for smiles of the biggest jerk in the world. He hadn't even opened his mouth yet, but that grin foretold that apologizing was the last thing he would do.

"You're right, man. It's not your fault. It's your *mamá's!*"

I have no idea how long it takes for a volcano to erupt, and I have no idea how long it takes for a tree to burst into flames when it's hit by a lightning bolt, but I certainly do know how long it takes for one of my dynamite cartridges to explode if you press the detonator—and what Marc did was jump up and down on it, right where it hurt most.

And, well, you need to know it takes very little time for me to explode, and by the avalanche of students that started to surround us, I guess the explosion must have been heard all over the mountain. I threw the snow in my hand on the ground, as if that might help me move faster, and I flew toward Marc. I know it's impossible I really flew, but I also swear I didn't touch the ground I was moving so fast. Marc remained frozen for a minute, but that didn't stop him and his friends from throwing a hundred snowballs at me to try to stop me. But gripped by fury as I was, that didn't do anything. Imagine me now with a black cloak, decked in leather, with sunglasses and my hair slicked back. I was in *The Matrix*, and I eluded every one of their missiles.

Nothing would stop me. Nothing stopped me.

Two leaps away from Marc, cocky bully that he was, I threw myself at him to knock him down. I don't know who first described snow as something smooth and soft, but when we fell to the ground, me on top of Marc, I could think only of the hard blow my knees had gotten and how cold and wet it was. Marc, in shock, didn't move, so I took advantage of that offensive moment as best I could. Immobilizing him with all my weight, I filled my hands with snow and stuffed his mouth with it.

"Shut up!" I shouted, adding a ton of expletives after that.

I could feel the stares of my friends, Jordi's troop, and our other classmates.

I was blind with rage.

Now I realize I should have kept quiet, that those words didn't help at all. I'm not saying that because of the insults themselves but because so much shouting at him knocked him out of his state of shock, and Marc started to defend himself. Snow and words were substituted by punches and slaps that desperately sought to find their goal, although they didn't manage to.

That attack of unbridled rage spread like a bruise. From that moment, as if only then did they realize what I had gotten myself into, some friends came to help me, although I don't know if they were coming to separate me from Marc or give him some punches with me. Other classmates started to fight among themselves. I heard two girls start to yell over a boy who surely wasn't worth it. I'd even swear that out of the corner of my eye I saw one teacher flailing away at another. But in reality I no longer saw or heard anything; I felt only my fist hitting Marc and my arm and a half trying to defend myself from his counterattacks.

Finally someone grabbed me under my arms and separated me from Marc. Only then did I realize what trouble I'd gotten myself into.

"Do you know what trouble you've gotten yourself into, young man?"

It was the gym teacher. Of course, he was the only one capable of picking me up as if I weighed less than a ski.

"Well, if I don't find my snowboard, I'm soon going to find out."

"And now you think you can act like a clown after beating up your classmate?"

"Oh, come on! We're not going to talk at all about how he said it was my mother's fault that I'm a damned cripple?"

He suddenly looked so surprised that I thought confetti would burst from his ears and a party horn from his mouth! Breaking news: Jordi's cronies were acting like real jerks! Yawn.

The rest of the teachers, however, weren't so willing to believe my version of the events, so for some forty minutes—much longer than it should have been and than I would have liked to endure—I seriously feared my goal of finishing ESO without a handful of disciplinary marks on my record had gone out the window.

All because I defended myself.

That afternoon, while I was seated in the lodge awaiting my possible punishment, I started to think of how that anger had spread so quickly inside me. How I, who had always tried not to let these things affect me too much, who always answered those absurd comments made to make me feel different with humor, had exploded and ended up so miserable.

Maybe I should've gone back to recover the spirit of the *rompecuellos* game, but how could I do that if my head went into red alert automatically, waiting for the next blow?

Luckily the teachers came to their senses and realized that, even if I hadn't acted properly, I wasn't really guilty. Not guilty that I was missing an arm or that Marc was a jerk. So they let me go and suspended Marc for a few days.

◆ ◆ ◆

After finishing my swimming exercises, I looked at my foot again in the shower. The bruise was there already, well defined, and had expanded beyond the impact where I'd hit the edge. That bit of skin would take on a yellowish tone rather than purple.

Yes, I had many more blows to endure. And the one from Marta really hurt me. It was one of the worst.

But I wouldn't give in.

I was always clear on that, since I was really little.

I had just forgotten it.

When I got home that afternoon, on the day when my heart was broken, it was never clearer to me. I just had to see the helicopter on my shelf to fully realize it.

I would fly high once more, so high no one would see the old David.

So the helicopter had the answer. And the solution?

Well, I still had to search a bit more inside myself.

PIECE BY PIECE

After Marta rejected me so elegantly, I spent a few days practically secluded in my room. Crying? Not exactly. I won't deny that I felt like it, but I wanted to focus my energies on other things.

But no spoilers—I've still got many things left to tell.

◆　◆　◆

During those days I didn't get too far on my crazy idea to build the new prosthesis. I just thought. I thought so much my head probably still hurts. But give me a few more chapters, and I'll tell you everything in the right order.

Before getting there, I should clarify it wasn't the first time I'd set myself up to attempt a project of such scope.

When I was nine years old, I'd already dabbled at being a little Dr. LEGOstein.

Back then I wanted to build myself a prosthetic arm. I had already thought the whole process through and, excited by the idea, I took the shell of the ship, the parts of some Bionicle robots, some duct tape, wiring, and the strap from a key chain that went around my neck. I put it together badly, took it apart, put it together better, and finished it. At the tender age of nine, I discovered the scientific method: trial and error. I would also discover that, no matter how many mistakes I made trying to make a plastic prosthetic, I wouldn't stop trying until I'd achieved it.

And when I did, I ran downstairs to show it to my parents.

"Mmmm . . . very nice," my mother said.

"Yes. Amazing, David!" my father exclaimed.

"What is that?" Naia asked.

They hadn't understood anything at all.

It's not like I'd explained much to them, I must admit.

What I had was a sort of rectangular box—gray and black, blue, red and white, with yellow trim—which had an opening at one end and at the other a kind of claw that resembled a hand. It could have been an orthopedic arm just the same as a satanic cornucopia or a somewhat sinister candlestick.

Without much more preamble, I'd pulled out the key chain strap I had kept hidden, put it around my neck to hold the prosthetic in place so it wouldn't fall from my *bracito*, and began to operate it. I even picked up objects with it for the first time.

"I made myself an arm!" I announced.

"Out of LEGOs?" Mamá asked. Her jaw began to drop. My father, for his part, had been knocked speechless.

"Yes, with the LEGOs you gave me. I took it apart and then put it together like this, and added in some other things."

"We've got a son who's far too clever!" Papá declared, getting up from the sofa and going right for his camera.

I felt swollen with pride just then and went back to my room. I paced circles around my prosthetic a thousand times, then around my bedroom a thousand times more, and finally decided to place it on my shelf. I pushed aside the little figures from the chocolate eggs to make space for it, and I set it down next to the spaceships and airplanes I had made from origami, another of my passions. I wanted the world to see the little things I had done and the big things I was starting to make. I had no idea what that moment was going to mean in my life and how the sails of that ship would carry me to terra firma in a not-too-distant future.

Impressed by that great feat and seeing how happy I'd felt just then, my parents encouraged me to bring it to school and show it to my classmates and teachers, although my mother had her doubts.

"Are you sure you want to bring it to school, David?"

I don't know if she was surprised or frightened, or if she just wanted to help me, but she was trying to make sure this was what I wanted or to decide if she should dissuade me from this mad path.

With the titanic LEGO prosthetic fixed to my right shoulder with the strap, I answered with an energetic, "Yes!"

My father, who insisted from the start I should take it to school, was very happy I was going to show off my achievement to everyone.

So whatever my mother's intention might have been, she was the only one who tried to dissuade me of anything.

"Of course he should, Nathalie. If he wants to bring it, let him bring it. I'm sure he'll impress all his teachers and classmates!"

He knew very well the admiration would give me a boost of confidence and raise my self-esteem, and that's what happened.

Soon after, I was on my way to school with my backpack and the prosthetic I had built. I admit I felt like a superhero—I was missing only my cape and a mask. LEGOman had arrived in town!

All the teachers appreciated it, and some made me talk about it, given that word had spread throughout the school. So I told everyone how I built it. At recess all my pals came to see the invention, and once more I explained the process for those who weren't in my classes.

"You look like a superhero!"

"You're too cool, David!"

"How amazing you made it all by yourself!"

"You're like a robot from the future!"

"You look like a junk pile," Jordi muttered. He had to live up to his role as idiot.

The truth is not everyone was into it. Some teachers looked at me strangely, with pity or concern—I don't know how to define it. And some of the other kids, not used to seeing me in the hallway, were even more surprised to see me at recess with a giant LEGO construction hanging from my arm than to see me with my *muñón* waving freely thanks to my specially tailored sleeves.

But I didn't care about any of that: not the eulogies, or the recognition, or the insults, or the looks of pity and incomprehension. What I was proud of was that I had managed to create it with my one hand and that I felt like I had two arms, even if one of them wasn't of any use other than taking up space and shining under the fluorescent lights of the hallways.

That day my mother got a call from the school psychologist. She wanted to meet with me to analyze whether that so-wonderful construction I'd made hid some psychological problem or even if it was a call for attention. My parents were calm because they knew the psychologist's fears couldn't be further from reality. They didn't doubt her good intentions and professionalism, so they decided it was fine for her to meet with me.

The interview took place (I'll go into it in more detail later), and it was concluded there was no problem.

"Your son is a whiz," the psychologist explained to my parents afterward. "David has considerable ability and enormous constructive capacities. It's very possible this prosthetic is the fruit of an important development achieved through his passion for building things."

Without a doubt it was something achieved thanks to my LEGO fanaticism, which would later lead to my big brick. Sorry, I meant to say my big *break*.

"And now what?" I asked myself after that day when I'd put the prosthetic back on the shelf.

What should I make now?

What was the big thing I would turn to next?

I would run down to the living room again and ask my parents to buy me another LEGO set. I'd build all of them, one by one, with just one hand.

It seemed like a solid plan, without any flaws.

Well, just one.

Money.

"OK, for Christmas we'll ask Santa Claus to bring you a new LEGO set to put together, the biggest one there is," Papá answered when I asked him.

I moved closer to him, making sure Naia wasn't near enough to hear me, and said, "You don't need to keep up all this Santa Claus nonsense with me, OK? Mamá was really angry when I tricked her about my homework that time, but you two have been pulling the wool over my eyes for years with Santa Claus and the Reyes Magos."

My father smiled, and although he loved my sense of humor, I couldn't twist his arm.

"We can't afford the extra expense, David. You'll have to wait until Christmas. Either that or get really good marks."

"How good?"

Still whispering, and with an ironic tone, he answered, "All tens."

I grimaced and turned around to head to my bedroom and stay there. Papá laughed. "Come on, David, money doesn't grow on trees."

"I know that! It comes from the bank!" I shouted. The bank also happened to be where he worked.

Back in my room, I looked at my prosthetic and picked it up. "Now what?" I once more asked myself, this time aloud.

Just then, holding the prosthetic, I realized how big a deal it really was. Seeing my parents' and classmates' stupefied joy, excitement, and wonder made me even more aware of what I had done. I must admit showing it off had helped me enormously.

With my hand, my *muñón*, my patience, and my dedication, I had built this thing without anyone's help. Who needed two arms? It was more fun to go through life like this, on the hard-difficulty level. The rewards were also better; the sense of satisfaction inside me was unlike anything else I'd experienced, and it wouldn't disappear, even if it might seem like a small eternity would pass before a new LEGO set fell into my hand.

I had a sudden flash. It was like a brief vision of what it might one day become. Would there be a day when I'd be able to build a much more realistic arm?

The idea, even though I'd wind up forgetting it for a few years, took root in my head just then. I had before me my next project: an enviable construction that, to my youthful eyes, would defy all the logic of human biology.

Given this thought, I decided to give myself time, because I still had lots more gifts to get. What if Abuela Basi or my aunt Diana gave me another set? I could practice even more and have even more pieces for my new project. After a bit more practice, nothing would stop me from seeing myself just like other kids.

The first time I found myself with a bunch of kids like me (but who had two arms), I felt strange and lost. I don't remember much more than the sensation of being afraid, being frightened. But the videos my father recorded during my first day of school speak for themselves and explain this and much more.

When I was very little, I spent a lot of time with my family, especially my *abuela*. We went to the park, and I played with other kids, but nobody was like me. The only reference I had was Peggy. I saw Dr. Doncel regularly on my medical visits, and I would have liked to have had more contact with my heroine, Peggy, but she was much older than me, basically another generation. No matter how much arm she was missing, I couldn't really identify with her. It was hard to see her as a reflection of me, as a companion. But there is no question Peggy helped me, because one way or another, she showed me I wasn't the only one in my situation.

So I thought there must have been other kids like me. Without realizing, in my imagination as a child of not yet four, I started to have a very clear fantasy: on the first day of school I would meet a boy or girl who was missing their left or right arm, just like me. I might even meet two kids like that.

"You're really eager to start school, aren't you? Do you know that's where big kids go?" all the adults were constantly asking me.

I energetically answered yes, because I wasn't afraid there were bigger kids at school. The only thing I cared about was meeting other kids my age and making friends.

You can imagine how nervous I was when the first day of school arrived. I was leaping all around the house and smiling from ear to ear. I felt like I was bursting with joy and anticipation.

"Is it time yet? Can we go? Is it now?" I kept repeating while Mamá chased after me to finish combing my hair and Papá recorded me with his camera. That's how I can remember the day, moment by moment, and all the crazy things I did—there's photographic proof.

And what proof it is!

When I reached the school, everyone could see how I was just beaming with excitement.

Despite there being a bunch of kids who were excited and nervous, and parents who didn't know what to do with so much free time ahead, and others who cried more than babies at being left alone, I stood out among all of them and not just because of my arm. There were so many children there, more than in any park I'd been in, that I didn't know where to start. Who should I approach first? Who seemed the nicest? Would they want to play ball? Which ones watched the same cartoons as me? Who else had just one arm or one leg or one hand?

But even at first glance I started to think I'd been wrong and my fantasy had been just that: a fantasy, nothing more, nothing less. Entering that patio outside the school and seeing so many arms gave me a stabbing feeling in my heart followed by a gentle whoosh. My chest deflated, and the joy spluttered out of me like air escaping from a small hole in a balloon. And just like the balloon, I zoomed through the air as I was deflating. (When I was little, I lived these situations very intensely. I still had to get used to the disappointments that only we humans are responsible for.)

I tried to deny what I saw at first. I took a spin around to try to meet someone. I wanted to play. I found a little group that seemed to get along, and I approached them. They stared at me strangely. I didn't know how to join them, and I ran away and took refuge between Papá's legs.

"What's the matter, David?" he asked, rubbing my head. I clutched his legs. "There are lots of kids. I'm sure you'll make a friend."

I wasn't so sure, but coming back to him, to the acceptance there'd always been at home, gave me renewed energy for my next attack.

Once more I approached another pair, a boy and a girl. Once more they looked at me strangely, and I didn't know how to integrate and ran back to my father.

"It's OK, champ." He rubbed my head again, and once more I started over.

I took a lot of spins around the patio, spoke with everyone, played with a few, and saw that no one was missing anything. They and their parents all saw I was missing an arm, and somehow I knew no one thought all of us were missing an eleventh finger. They were all surprised to see me. Some were afraid, and others were amazed looking at my right arm, almost as if they were jealous. I tried not to let it show that they made me feel uncomfortable, that I didn't like to be the center of attention like that. This was not like the *rompecuellos* game; this was very different. I'd have to see these kids every day. I wasn't crossing paths with them once in our lifetime, like with passersby. So when the shame and fear gripped me, I always ran to clutch Papá's legs.

The only thing I wanted was to have friends, no matter how many arms they had. It was that simple, with no complications, right? I wanted to play with them, laugh with them, be like them, and for no one to stare at me, not with disgust, or with pity, or with fear. That first day of school was terrifying precisely because everything was new for me and my classmates, and for them it was the same to meet someone like me. I'd asked, like the innocent kid I was, for too much in too short a time.

Sure enough I eventually learned the disgust, pity, and fear belonged more to the parents than to the kids. For them it was enough that I knew how to play *pica paret* or tag.

"Why are you missing an arm?"

"I was born that way."

"How strange. All the kids I know have two arms like me."

"Yes. All the ones I know also have two arms."

"Is there no one else like you, then?"

"Yes, but they're already older."

"Cool. You wanna kick the ball together?"

Conversations usually followed this path, and although during those early years I got excited when everything worked out and we started to play, over time I got fed up with these kinds of questions and comments. It didn't matter that it was always their first time seeing someone like me; for me it was like living Groundhog Day for the umpteenth time.

When you introduce yourself to someone, you say your name, what grade you're in, what you're studying, what hobbies you like, and little more, right? Usually that's enough. At most you might talk about your favorite shows, the classes you have in common, the exam in algebra last week . . . It's never been like that for me. The missing arm always seems to matter more than my own name.

"Wow, you're missing an arm!"

"How observant," I'd sometimes joke.

"What happened to you?"

"A shark bit off my arm when I tried to save my sister."

"Yowza! And is she OK?" they'd ask right after an inevitable pause to catch their breath.

"My sister? Yes, but you should see how I left the shark."

At that point they'd start to doubt the veracity of my story, and I could tell by their look of confusion they were wondering if I was trying to put one over on them. But in reality what's happened is I've left them exposed. Other times I bring the joke to an end after the obligatory pause leaves them completely discombobulated.

I started this tactic too late, after the *colonias* of second year of ESO. My life would've been much more fun if I'd put it into practice sooner. After the fright I gave those boys and girls from the other school when they arrived on the bus, some of them sought me out to tell me that it had been really cool and that at first they were really frightened.

"You're a natural! It was better than any Tunnel of Terror!"

Of course, then came the eternal question: "What happened to your arm?"

Why couldn't I turn those *colonias* into three really fun-filled days?

"A lion ate it when I was on safari with my parents."

"I was bitten by a crocodile, and they had to amputate it."

"There's this really venomous spider, and if it bites you . . ."

"If you say *manco* seven times in front of the mirror at midnight . . ."

"I got run over by a truck when I tried to save a kitten, and I lost my arm."

"Well, you see, I was biting my nails. And the thing is, sometimes once you start, you just don't stop."

"Oh, it was a silly accident I had."

"You know when your mother tells you not to lick the knife after spreading Nutella? Well . . ."

I could think of thousands of stories like these, each more absurd, ridiculous, unlikely, and fun than the one before. Although I suppose I was the one having the most fun with it. I spread around three different versions at those *colonias* after my second year of ESO, and I turned into the biggest mystery the students at that school had ever met.

First encounters are always hard, and the first day is always the hardest—at school, at high school, and even at university. But I found that humor smooths the path and makes everything simpler and lighter, both for others as well as for myself. The pressure evaporates, and the weight of the backpack you're carrying lightens a bit. The others begin to take back the "books" they've given you, and suddenly you feel like you're floating. Everything becomes much easier.

But on that first day of school, I could barely have imagined all that. I went from my father to my classmates, wandering in circles, jumping, trying to act like the others, fearing getting rejected so many times it's astonishing to count them all in the photos and video of "David's First Day of School." There came a moment when I was so tired, I don't know if physically or mentally I stood staring at my own reflection in the glass doors.

My father showed me that video again a little while ago to refresh my memory of my childhood. I didn't remember that moment looking at the doors. In fact I still don't. What was going on? What was going through my head? Maybe I was seeing myself for the first time as different from everyone, really different. Maybe I was sad because nobody seemed to want to play with me. Maybe I had decided I didn't like school. Maybe I thought only of wanting to go home, to be with my *abuela*, to wake up from a siesta in her lap and see her reading *Pronto* with the television on low so it didn't wake me. Maybe I remembered only sweet moments, or maybe I could already foresee bitter moments to come.

It was not an easy day.

Now I realize that, perhaps, when I decided to construct the prosthetic with the ship, I unconsciously remembered that day and how I saw myself in the glass door, with the happy and whole children running all around me. And how if I had to show the world I wasn't missing anything, I would build a prosthetic myself. I could do it. I could build it, put it on, try it, and use it or not use it. Because although I could, I didn't *need* to use it.

Just me, the way I was born, was enough.

THE TALE
OF
HAND SOLO

Check out these photos from my life.

Ferran and David, two pretty cool dudes.
(Photo by José Sánchez, Foto Estudi La Seu)

My origin story: Here's little me. As you can see,
I've always been handsome.

(Photo by José Sánchez, Foto Estudi La Seu)

My family is everything.

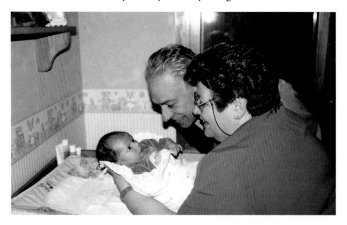

Here's Abu Basi and Juan, my grandparents, welcoming baby me.

The four of us: Mamá, Papá, me, and Naia.

The annual family trip to Menorca.

Playing with Papá.

LEGO love then and now:

My first trip to LEGOLAND
in Denmark. I am completely unable to contain myself!

A personal gift to me from Craig Glenday, *Guinness World
Records* editor—so incredible to see myself as a LEGO!

Some of my creations:

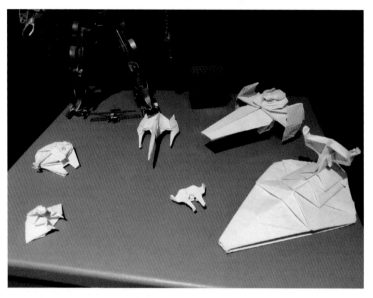

Check out my origami game.

Me with the MK-2 and LEGO jet plane.

From left to right: MK-1 through MK-5. Who would have thought that my LEGO creation at age nine would take me here? (Photo by Miquel Liso)

Even when you're an international star, it's important to keep a sense of humor. (Photo by Marcos Saavedra Seoane)

Here I am at NASA(!) with Charlie Wen (left), cofounder and former head of Marvel's Visual Development department at Marvel Studios, and my mentor Dimitris Bountolos (center), senior advisor of NASA Cross-Industry Innovation Summit. (Courtesy Dimitris Bountolos)

A little friendly competition between father and son. We took this photo to help promote the music in my documentary, *Mr. Hand Solo*. (Photo by José Sánchez, Foto Estudi La Seu)

I was psyched to win on *LEGO Masters* France, with my partner Sébastien Mauvais. (Courtesy Sébastien Mauvais)

Here I am, super excited about receiving a Guinness World Record for creating the first functional LEGO prosthetic arm.

Looking fancy at my country's first Ibero-American Summit, where I had the opportunity to present. I was so honored to be a part of it!

I'm completely floored to have been included in *National Geographic Spain*, and to be photographed by the amazing photographer Pau Fabregat.

Did I mention that a documentary was made about my life?
Here we are, living the dream.

Papá and I posing with the Spanish edition of our book (the book you're holding now in English translation!). We're officially authors! (Photo courtesy Josep Segura/Grup Dona Secret S.L.)

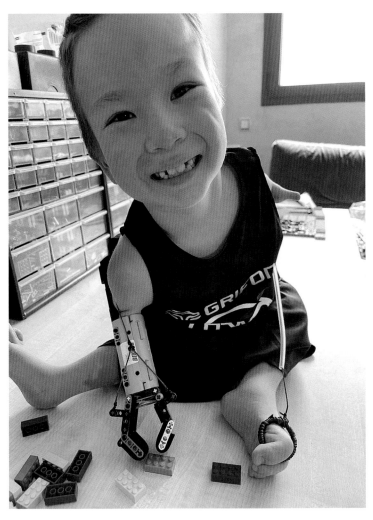

Beknur Zhanibekuly from Kazakhstan wearing a LEGO prosthetic designed by me, named the MK-Beknur.

Papá and me, still designing, still dreaming.

I don't see anything missing here, do you?
(P.S. Thanks, Papá, for the sweet wheels.)

NO RORSCHACH TEST

Even today I can't help but smile when I remember how my parents stared at me when I showed them the first prosthetic I made. That one had taken me a long time to build, and as you've seen, I finished it with less secrecy and planning. I just kept building and trying, building and trying . . .

It was a great experiment, even if the school psychologist wound up calling me in to talk to her as a result. Now I need to tell you something, and you need to believe me, despite the chronology of events, OK? Before finishing class and getting the call to see the psychologist, I'd already decided the next day I wouldn't wear the titanic arm to school. In fact I had even thought about what I could turn it into next. There was a LEGO helicopter I knew my family wouldn't get me for a long time, so I thought to make one myself. I'd turn the masts of the sails into the helicopter blades, and for the landing skids I'd use . . .

"Did I get myself into trouble?" I asked as I entered the psychologist's office.

She assured me everything was fine and I didn't need to worry about anything. She just wanted to ask me a few questions that, to tell the truth, I didn't really understand. Did she want me to stop creating things? Why was she so interested in my prosthetic? It was something good! Wasn't it?

I left the office pretty confused. But I knew I had done nothing wrong, and the psychologist hadn't tried to pressure me.

But what if she had interpreted my construction as a call for help? Perhaps I might have started to hide my *muñón* (as I later did when I was a teen), or I'd have put the LEGOs together only the way the box indicated, not dared to continue experimenting with the Bionicles, and never become interested at all in the modifications of the bike, the superbike, and the superbike 2.0.

I'll let you know I should have trusted the psychologist more, because as I've already told you, everything was fine. The truth was she was amazed by my abilities. After my parents explained everything to me, I decided to keep going with my LEGO building, full speed ahead. I couldn't wait to be given even more construction sets!

It turned out the psychologist was alarmed because of other signs of "calling for help" that I seemed to have shown, like a short story we were asked to write for class with a Christmas theme. Mine was about a boy who was missing an arm, and for Christmas he decided to ask for one from Santa Claus. His parents, when they heard him ask the mall Santa for one and read it in the letter he wanted to mail to Santa, tried to dissuade him, because they knew Santa couldn't bring it. However, the boy's faith was so strong the next day he woke up with two arms, and the entire family embraced happily, recovering the Christmas spirit and belief in the magic of Christmas.

What's so funny about that, you ask? The fact my mother had helped with my homework that day! I had gotten so worried and upset about the assignment that in the end she just wrote it for me. The story seemed cute and saccharine to me, so I turned it in without thinking about it anymore. As surprising as it might seem, neither one of us imagined it might come off as strange or be misinterpreted. My nonexistent *bracito* is part of our everyday, and we were so used to it this story just seemed kind of quaint to us.

The psychologist was left speechless when my parents explained all this to her. Her job was to make sure everything was going well and, if not, to help us. She was always very attentive and professional, and at no time did she

question my parents' love and care for me. A very typical
mistake when we go to therapy is thinking the psychologist
is playing against us.

Luckily, in my case, I didn't have those fears. Nor did
we think there was anything wrong. She had asked me how
I felt with the attention of my classmates, and she wanted
to know why I'd brought the prosthesis to school. I told
her the truth, of course. "I wanted my friends to see it. My
constructions always stay behind in my room, in my home.
I don't know, I was excited."

"Do you make other constructions, David?"

"Lots of them. I'm always asking to get LEGOs for my
birthday. Yesterday the prosthesis was a pirate ship, and
now I want to turn it into a helicopter or plane, because I
know it will be ages before I'm given another one. Since my
birthday has already passed for this year . . ."

"You do everything by yourself with your one hand?"

"Yes."

"And what else do you like to do?"

"You mean making things? Origami!"

As I've told you, it wasn't clear if I was getting into
trouble or not. But that same afternoon, after their phone
conversation with the psychologist, my parents assured me
nothing was wrong and I wasn't in any trouble. It was not
until a few years later that they explained the full story to

me and the misunderstanding that had taken place after I made what would become the MK-1, a prosthetic that was much more functional than the first one although not as sophisticated as the others I'd make later.

Yes, you've guessed it.

Just as the LEGO pirate ship had helped me make that vital earlier experiment, the helicopter I stared at on the afternoon my heart was broken would have a second life, too, as my most famous LEGO arm.

THE SADDEST SUMMER OF MY LIFE

Marta broke my heart, and I almost broke the door. The door to my bedroom.

By slamming it.

The helicopter trembled on its shelf, and that's why I looked at it. It was next to the arm.

"*. . . don't want to go out with you. You're missing an arm and . . .*"

"*Why did you bring the prosthesis to school?*"

"*It's not your fault. It's your* mamá's!"

"*You're like a robot from the future!*"

"*Do you think it's going to spin?*"

I hit the helicopter's blades with one finger, and they began to spin and spin and spin, like the memories in my head. The voices of my parents, my classmates, Marc, Marta . . . echoing one after another in the corners of my mind, leaving no space for anything else. They were like the buzzing of a thousand honeybees battling against a thousand bumblebees. My head was like a hive, and my heart was like a wasp's nest.

What happened with Marta was the detonator of a whole chain of events that left me more and more broken down. They say bad things come in threes. That day I thought I'd learned what it felt like for someone to break your heart. But that's not quite true. It was already broken in pieces, from all the hurtful words and questions that had come before.

When you fall, even if you need to rest, it's pretty easy to get back up. You need time. But what happens when you're broken into a thousand shards?

For years now I think of that summer and holiday break as a broken piece of glass, the color of turquoise and pale as the winter sun. Its bits are scattered across the floor, and if I bend down, I see they neither return my reflection nor let me see the ground beneath them, because each fragment of glass reflects a different year and summer.

I pick up one of the shards, and I see myself at four years old, playing in the pool with Papá at the summer house in Menorca. Mamá is sitting on the edge of the pool, with her feet in the water, and she laughs at Papá's foolishness. That was the year I learned to swim.

I leave that piece in its place and pick up another one. This time I see the whole family on the ferry that takes us to the island, and Naia, nine years old already, poses in front of an orange ring buoy and smiles. Every year on our summer trip to Menorca we repeat that photo, with the same poses. So you can see every change, every tiny difference in our expressions, hairstyles, faces.

My attention shifts now to another shard, and I see myself folding a piece of paper on itself a hundred times. Now here, now there, I fold this edge, I unfold this other. I must be six or eight, and beside me unfolds a vast arsenal of weapons made from paper: a pistol, a rifle, blowtubes I'd later use in all sorts of pranks. Every neighbor surely knew the conical bullets lost in their garden, on their balcony or terrace, or in any of the parks of the neighborhood belonged to me, that they had been propelled from one of my multiple paper weapons. Give me a package of sheets of paper, and I'd defeat any army with skill, paper, and a single arm.

I put that shard back in its place and slide my attention to another. I'm on the beach, with my parents and sister. Naia's still a baby, and it's the first time we're bringing her to the beach.

Despite how often my parents insisted I go in the water, I remained under the umbrella, because even wearing sunblock, I turn red in the sun and burn right away. "I don't want to! I don't want to!" The algae and bits of reeds in the water disgust me. They're like dead things, and I panic whenever they touch my legs, as if they might be jellyfish that could tear them off or leave them useless. I start to imagine this must be what happened with my *bracito* when I was very, very little, so little I don't even remember, and my parents kept it hidden from me as some evil joke between the two of them.

My imagination keeps returning to that afternoon. I start to do origami for the first time, by myself, bored because Papá and Mamá and Naia are asleep, and on TV there are only movies about kidnappings. I fold the paper without quite knowing what I'm doing, yet knowing exactly how to do it. Just like with the pieces of the figures, I follow the points of light and the vibration. My intuition guides me and whispers to me how and where I should fold and which way to unfold. Trial and error. Attempt and discard. And start over again.

One of the shards starts to shine intensely, blurring the reflection that has caught me. I put the piece down, careful not to cut myself on the edges, and pick up the other. As soon as my eyes catch its reflection, I know why it shone that way. I see my *abuela* Basi, reading *Pronto* on her sofa, Naia and I on the other side of the couch, stuffed and sound asleep after the huge feast she'd prepared for us. It's the early days of summer, when my parents were still working and left us with Abu. She takes us to the park in the morning, then I play with Naia while Basi prepares lunch, then we have a siesta on the sofa. Mamá comes to pick us up in the afternoon, and together we all go to the bank to get my father. There are nights when Abu Basi stays at our house for dinner, and the next morning we're left at her house once more. She makes breakfast for us with affection—there's always something with chocolate—and that's how each day passes until the vacation time arrives, when we come down from Andorra to catch the ferry to Menorca and swim and sunbathe.

Those memories are the ones that repeat again and again in my head that day at the cemetery, surrounded by my whole family.

My whole family except for her.

It was time for us to say goodbye.

Tears slid down my cheeks like silent, unceasing waterfalls. They sprang from a well of pain that, sealed off until then, now seemed to find its way out. I had cried on only three occasions in my life up till then, and my *abuela*'s funeral was, without a doubt, the worst of all. I didn't dare raise my eyes from the ground for even a second. Seeing the whole scene or catching the eyes of any of my relatives would only have made my devastating grief break the sky. But what broke at that moment were the memories of all my summers, forever stained by the bitter taste of the heat and dazzling sun, with no shade to shelter in, that morning at the cemetery.

When the ceremony was over, the wave of dark sunglasses and black clothes I found myself in said an affectionate farewell with hugs and kisses and dispersed at the gates. Wrapped in a sort of emotional fog, we went home without speaking a word. Papá drove, Mamá kept a sepulchral silence, and Naia rested her head against the window. I don't know why, but I couldn't stop scratching my stump. It was itching like crazy. Tears threatened to overwhelm my eyes once more when I remembered how when I was little, Abu Basi kept tucking me in with the swaddling cloth she'd sewn for me, even after I had long outgrown it, how she'd said goodbye by giving a little squeeze to the tiny hand of my *muñón* ever since I asked her not to say goodbye with a kiss because "I was too old for that now." Perhaps I was also too stupid, I thought, arriving home and throwing myself on my bed.

Not even after doing many laps in the pool or after a phys ed class, trying to keep up with my classmates, had I ever felt so exhausted. It was a weariness so vast I noticed how, even while I took off the heavy suit from the funeral, it wanted to make a tiny ball out of me that didn't move for days. Once I managed to shower, I didn't fight against the strength of that weariness. I threw myself on my bed and fell asleep with the hope of putting an end to the nightmare, hoping it would all be a bad dream that would be over after a little nap.

That was just the beginning.

When I woke up, not only did I have to grapple with the fact that, no, it hadn't just been a nightmare, but also that I had to face everyday life without my *abuela*. She had accepted me from the first moment, since she saw my father weeping in that hospital. She always had something to say, strength to keep going, and love to give. Could the world go on like before, without so strong and tireless a woman, who'd given everything for us?

No.

But life wasn't going to stop.

So every day I got up to go to class, endured the pity of my classmates and Marta's elusive gaze whenever our paths crossed, and studied as much as my head allowed. The MK-1 project was tucked away in a box, and I thought about it very little, and when I did it was to consider it something stupid, like the biggest foolishness I'd ever thought of. What did I think I would do with a LEGO arm? Why didn't I go right to an orthopedist? Maybe, if it was still open, the one whose pamphlet appeared in our mailbox that day I came home from the hospital might still have offerings available for us.

It was then that my grades started to plummet until they settled lower than five in all my classes. Even physics and math. Even Catalan, Castilian, history. The heat arrived with increasing violence, but I still wore long sleeves and tucked the right cuff into my pocket. My teachers called my parents, and my parents spoke with me. I tried, studied, and struggled to concentrate, but my head rejected anything that tried to enter it. There was no room left. The wound from Marta's betrayal kept bleeding. The well of grief my *abuela* had left behind seemed impossible to drain. In the end I had to put on short sleeves because the heat won, and I had to repeat five subjects.

María put up with me during the entire walk home.

"Your parents won't kill you," she tried to console me.

After what happened with Marta, María became one of my best friends and confidants. It was always better to talk about things like this with a girl your own age than with your mother. Although Mamá helped me a lot, there were things I couldn't explain to her. And now María helped me with my Fs.

"I'm going to repeat the second year of *bachillerato*, and I won't go to university." I sighed. "If they don't kill me, they'll want to cut off my other arm."

María laughed. "They won't do that. Don't you see then you wouldn't be able to do the makeup exams?"

I sighed with disgust. I hadn't remembered about the September tests.

"And on top of everything, I'll wind up with no summer vacation because I'll have to study!"

After everything that had happened that year, I was in no mood to go to Menorca or make some special trip to the Canary Islands or Malta like we'd done in other years. None of us felt like it. It would be a quiet summer at home, with long days to be with family, watch movies or series, and meet up with the few friends who weren't spending those months out of town. I could take advantage of the time to go out on my bike, which I'd neglected for weeks and weeks. I could even, if I felt like it, resume building the MK-1. But instead of all that, the only thing I'd be doing would be sticking my butt in a chair and carving two holes in the desk with my elbows while I studied like never before.

Were my parents going to kill me? Would they tear off my other arm as I had said? To be completely honest, I took longer than usual to tell them. How much longer, exactly? So long that in reality I didn't tell them myself. They saw it on my report card.

"Comment est-ce possible?" I heard my mother from the other end of the house. Of course I didn't hand the report card to her directly. I "forgot" it on the table in the entryway, in the hopes one of the two of them would notice it. "David, *viens ici tout de suite!*"

Just hearing her in French, I knew what was in store for me. When I arrived, it was my father who was staring at my grades. My mother stood beside him with her arms crossed. She kept speaking in French. "David, do you know if this is some error?"

I didn't answer. I couldn't.

"Five classes, David," my father continued.

"You promised you were going to make an effort."

"Five!"

"It must be an error, no? That's so many, I'm sure that . . ."

"No, it's not an error," I confessed at last.

Not that there was much left to confess; everything was spelled out clearly on that piece of paper. I explained to them how bad all my final exams had gone despite my efforts, and how I'd managed to trick my teachers so they

didn't meet with them during the final days of class. I didn't
do it out of selfishness or fear that my parents would find
out the whole truth. They'd already had meetings at the
beginning of the trimester, when everything already was
pointing toward disaster. I did it so they wouldn't worry
even more. The family had so much to deal with, starting
with the huge event that had knocked our lives sideways.
Why add another problem when there was nothing to be
done about it, when everything already depended on my
luck in September? I wanted to delay the unpleasantness for
them as long as possible. Bad things come in threes, they
say, but at least let there be a bit of time between one and
the next so they could rest and recover.

That's how I explained myself. But that appeased their
anger only over my silence—not for the five failed subjects.
After all, the entire degree and my university future were at
risk. I, David Aguilar Amphoux, the boy who had sworn
he could do anything he set himself to, was about to repeat
a year of school.

"This summer we won't go anywhere," my father
declared. Not like we were in the mood, but my grades
were the straw that broke the camel's back. "We'll help you
study, David. We'll organize a plan of study. We'll make a
schedule so you can rest and not feel like you're losing your
vacation, and starting in August we can look for a private

tutor to give you a hand. You'll see. You won't repeat the year, and you'll get the highest notes of the second exam seating. You can't lose this experience with all your friends. With Álex, María, Pep . . ."

But was it truly terrible if I did miss it?

So what if I repeated a year?

So what if my classmates left me behind?

It wasn't as if I couldn't complete my *bachillerato* ever again.

It wasn't as if my friends and I would stop talking to one another just because I repeated a year.

There were people who got their *bachillerato* in four years. Or who got it as an adult. Or who went to university when they were forty. Or who studied long distance because they needed to work at the same time.

What if now wasn't my moment?

And I had to wait a little?

And if, aware of my mistake, what I *wanted* was to repeat the year so I'd arrive at university as well prepared as possible?

And if . . . ?

Maybe that option existed. To fall down, rest, get better, and keep going. Maybe now was the moment of healing, of stopping the hemorrhage of the wound, of draining the well of pain little by little to avoid a total collapse. Perhaps it was time to take things calmly, sit and take deep breaths, and prepare for battle, better and with more strength. Nothing happened because a person repeated a grade; on the contrary, it could be an advantage. I could learn better, more calmly, and at my own rhythm. It could prepare me better for the entrance exams and university.

It wasn't the moment to force myself. That's how I started to feel in July, when the study sessions seemed longer and longer to me, unbearably tedious and less fruitful with every second. My friends had already taken the entrance exams and knew if they had gotten into the degree program they wanted to study, if they had to challenge their results or maybe look for a private university. Meanwhile, I sank my elbows into the desk and tried not to grow dizzy over my notes. The heat, grief, and pressure from my family made everything I studied, or tried to study, stretch like a bubblegum bubble instead of becoming fixed in my memory, growing thinner and weaker until finally bursting and all that remained of it were a few ridiculous splotches splattering what I had written in the textbooks and my notes.

My fate was to fail. But I couldn't get that into my father's head.

"David, you can't lose a year," he insisted. "If you put effort into it, you'll pass and manage to take the entrance exams with all the subjects fresh in your mind."

"But I barely understand the subjects now," I tried to reason—without much success, I'll let you know. "I'll get worse results. I won't be able to matriculate for the degree I want!"

"Don't be so defeatist. With that attitude we won't get anywhere. Besides, all roads lead to Rome. You could start a different degree and then validate the classes."

"Isn't that losing a year? Starting one degree I don't want in order to save two classes? Two if I'm lucky! If I pass them!"

"Come on! You'll do much better at university. Don't compare it with what we're going through now. You can do anything, *hijo*."

"Sure, like passing year two of *bachillerato*, no?"

Like the water that splashes against the edge of the pool, I crashed against my father over this. As I swam to keep up with my physical exercise and keep air out of my head after studying, I thought about how to convince him his path was not the best option for me. In part because of my current state and in part because of how university would be for me if I entered in fits and starts or started a degree that wasn't what I wanted to study. Was it that I could hardly see the future I wanted to pursue? Without even mentioning the dangers of the second tests, there were fewer university slots left, the cutoff point for grades would change, and everything would all go to you-know-where. But above all I was losing a summer to studying. Three months of sweating and stress, note-taking, and air-conditioning, during which the only water I swam in was the pool, and not for fun but to do my exercises, and on top of everything I had to put up with my sister complaining that we hadn't gone on vacation because of me.

I don't think Papá understood the pressure I was under, how difficult that summer was proving to be for me. Some demons that had pursued me over the course of my life had caught me, and among other things, it was the first time I faced the grief of losing someone. And let's not forget I was betting the school year and my whole future on three months of summer. We were all going through a really tough time, and it was normal that we wanted everything to get back to normal so we could recover our usual routines as quickly as possible. Repeating a year was an unexpected tributary that opened before us, and while it seemed better to avoid it, I wasn't so sure it would be something bad. Maybe it was the path I needed to take. Perhaps, in the end, the tributary was in reality the main watercourse, and it would lead me to the sea I was hoping to reach. Sometimes the unexpected holds the biggest solutions in life, and to achieve them, we just need to let ourselves follow the current.

Now, not everything was long hours of studying, arguments with my father, burst bubblegum bubbles, and exercises in the pool. After a daily ration of each of those stellar moments, night found me with my Launchpad and my headphones. Once I put them on, nothing else existed except the music and me. Note by note, I constructed the music I heard behind my ears. With the music I tried (although I wouldn't manage to achieve it) to consolidate everything I'd studied, and it relaxed me before going to bed and facing the next day's notes.

There was also the yellow helicopter on its shelf, unaware of what it would be transformed into and the fact it would change my life. It watched me with pity and patience, as if it knew it had to wait for my fingers to turn it into what it was destined to be.

That complex LEGO toy was the only thing that kept my patience until the end of that stifling summer. One afternoon Papá and I got into an epic argument that isn't worth repeating here. Angry, I put a halt to that absurd exchange of words by going up to my bedroom and loudly slamming the door. Once there I threw my notebooks and textbooks on the floor, blind with rage, pulled out the Launchpad, and devoted the rest of the day to composing, with the windows open so a bit of air came in, my headphones on and completely ignoring my parents, who tried to come into my bedroom to "speak about what had just happened."

I didn't want to talk.

I wanted to do what I thought was best for me.

What I *needed*.

They had always supported me in my decisions. When I had decided to go to the *colonias* for the first time. When I decided to go again during ESO. When I decided not to go on the kayaking trip. When I decided to try more sports. When I decided to study a technology *bachillerato*.

I couldn't understand why their position had changed so radically now. I guess extracurricular choices were one thing, and having my academic life in checkmate was another. But nothing bad would happen from repeating; on the contrary, it could help me.

"We want the best for you, David," my father explained to me days later when I had calmed down from our fight. I was starting to feel very nervous because the first recovery exam was just two weeks away now, and my head still felt like a sponge—not the kind that can absorb things but one of those loofah ones from the shower, dry and unable to absorb anything. "The other day we got a bit intense, and we shouldn't have reached that point. We don't want you to lose an academic year and—"

"But, Papá, it wouldn't be losing it, it would be—"

"Taking advantage of it to the maximum. I know. That's why I wanted to tell you . . ." He seemed to hesitate, but in a sure tone he continued, "That if you wind up repeating a year, there's nothing wrong. In the end it'll be for the best. But you need to try first, OK?"

"In other words it's OK if I make a faux pas instead of a pass?" I joked.

"Don't push your luck." He laughed. "Now go up to your room and put some effort into it. There's not much time left. Do what you can without giving up, *hijo*."

"Like I always do!"

"Like always."

My father realized he had pushed things to the breaking point with me and reacted accordingly.

Seriously, my parents had always been very firm in supporting my decisions. I'd always been the one who didn't give up. I kept going, with or without rest, with or without wounds. And I always reached the goal, no matter in what position. Because if I had a target, I didn't stop until I managed to hit it.

At some point along the path I had traveled the past few months, I'd forgotten that. I'd settled down to sleep, and it was time to move on.

But I couldn't get up.

Don't be nervous, mi niño. *You'll pass everything. You can do everything.* That's what Abuela Basi would tell me if she were still here with us. I knew that clearly.

I felt how she embraced me.

That's what gave me the strength I needed to get up and continue with my head held high, no matter the result.

And when everything was over, it would be time to settle a debt I had waiting.

The helicopter watched me during those final days of study without rest. You could almost say it urged me on.

I'VE ALREADY LIVED THROUGH THIS

In the end I didn't pass three subjects.

I guess that's why I keep repeating that bad things come in threes.

It wasn't too hard a blow for me, though. It was much worse for my parents to handle. Despite their fervent desire to accept whatever happened, they couldn't help but show their disappointment when I told them I hadn't managed to make up all my subjects. I'd have to repeat the year, and university entrance exams would once more be something abstract and part of a future that seemed to never arrive. After that my parents became almost indulgent in every-thing, as if I was the one who was more disappointed and frustrated. Mamá prepared my favorite dish to console me, Papá helped me repair the wheel of my bike that had gotten a flat on my way to one of the exams, and my sister promised to do all my chores for a week (although she lasted only two days).

For my part I was calm. Relaxed. I felt like my *abuela* had accompanied me over these past few days and I had managed to do all I was capable of right now. Even though I didn't get a chance to shout "Bingo," passing in two subjects that I'd been failing at all year was nothing to sneeze at, and I felt proud to have done so, especially because I'd been in such a funk when I'd studied. I don't wish it on anyone to be grieving at the same time as preparing for makeup exams.

When I got my grades, with my passes and fails, the yellow LEGO helicopter looked at me with expectation. I could tell how it wanted me to take it down from the shelf and get to work, with my notebook of designs at my side.

"Not yet" was all I sighed.

It's hard to explain, but it still wasn't the right moment. I looked at the helicopter, revised my notes in the notebook, but I didn't see those tones and lights I always did when I was constructing something. It was as if suddenly I didn't even know how to fit one piece to the next, as if I'd lost all ability to build figures in their potential essence. Something was missing, and I didn't know what.

So I left it resting.

The whirlwind of events I found myself in over the next weeks helped distract me and even contributed to my forgetting about the MK-1.

A few weeks after learning I would repeat my second year of *bachillerato*, school started up again. Even though that meant I didn't need to buy new textbooks this year, I still had to prepare for the start of the *old* school year. I needed pens, notebooks, a new scientific calculator, set squares for technical drawing (preferably ones that weren't broken), and to mentally prepare myself for meeting new people. I needed to get a lot ready in record time, and some things were harder to get than others.

Andorra is small, and the school I went to even smaller. That means, in some way or another, we all knew one another—this person in fourth is the cousin of the girl from second, the guy from third is the son of the owner of the corner supermarket, the one from A is the sister who graduated with honors last year, the girl from first is the oldest child of the chemistry teacher . . . I could almost draw a map of connections between all the students at school and their families. But even if I could do that, I wouldn't really *know* them, not like I would after having gone to school together for more than ten years.

And that made me nervous.

The only advantage I had was that, just like I knew them as "the cousin of the owner of the dealership" or "the older sister of my sister's best friend," for them I was "David, the guy who's missing an arm" or "David, who made himself a LEGO arm when he was nine," or maybe, "the oldest child of the man from the bank—yeah, the one who doesn't have an arm."

At least I wouldn't need to go through the usual introductions. And thanks to being a repeater, I felt sure the teachers wouldn't make me introduce myself in front of the entire class as if I were some odd duck arrived from another school.

Or so I thought.

Some teachers had the clever idea of announcing to the class that for this *new* year we had among us a new incorporation to the class, a kid for whom the entire syllabus should be *familiar*. It was a good thing I was repeating only the subjects I'd failed. Needless to say, that was a delicate way of introducing me as a failed student. Good job! I was sure to earn friends right away . . . the loser repeater who was missing an arm.

But they were also missing an eleventh finger. And perhaps in some cases a more empathetic brain.

Despite the brutality of those introductions, none of that affected me too much. Yes, I wanted to get along with my new classmates, to have friends to study with in the library and exchange notes with, but also to go to their parties on the weekends and have a good time—in short, to enjoy typical school life. And to pass, and move on, and prepare myself properly to get into university. I couldn't lose sight of my goal or forget why I'd found myself living this continuous déjà vu.

The first days were the most boring. The syllabus was, indeed, quite familiar. It was like waking up from a dream and seeing everything clearly for the first time. Then, during recess, I went out to the street and to the cafeteria, where I always had breakfast with María. Luckily that time period coincided with her break between classes, so we held a video chat. I had a great time with her like always, but in some ways I couldn't help feeling she'd left me behind—especially because she was in another city, at her university, and I saw her only through a screen. She explained to me everything that any second-year *bachillerato* student wanted to know about the uni, but to a repeater like me it felt like a stabbing pain just below his chest. Like how university teachers were so laid-back about everything and didn't care if you arrived late to class or drank coffee in the middle of a lesson, so long as you didn't interrupt or make noise. She even knew the dates for her first midterms already, plus the deadlines for when work needed to be turned in for the entire semester. It was thrilling and at the same time ter-rifying. It was a new student life, completely different from what we'd lived until then, which needed to be adjusted to, with its pros and cons.

Given how lousy my second year of *bachillerato* had gone for me, without a doubt it would have been worse to have kept pushing forward with the entrance exams and enter university. By repeating, I had avoided a derailment that quite possibly could have blown up everything I'd been working toward. I might not have been able to rise up again from that fall.

So despite my boredom and feelings of abandonment, it confirmed what I already knew:

I had made the right decision.

I had done what needed to be done.

That opened something new in my chest that drowned out the piercing envy and longing I sometimes felt. My sit-uation had its inconveniences, for sure, but also its advan-tages. I didn't manage to identify that pleasant emotion that seemed to underpin every step I took and encouraged me to raise my hand in class and take part actively. I just knew it made me feel good, and that was enough. Thanks to it, I dared to talk to my new classmates, and they felt encour-aged to approach me. I began to make friends and had more and more desire to go to class. The homework didn't feel so heavy, and I heard a melody every time I looked at the helicopter on the shelf. But the first exams came as Halloween was approaching, and I had to focus on them. I feared having to once again confront the subjects I'd failed at the beginning of September. They were my baptism by fire. Another obstacle to overcome.

One ordinary day, the teacher showed up with our corrected exams and started passing them out to us. When she gave me mine, my heart almost stopped. I couldn't believe the grade I'd gotten: I'd passed! I could succeed. I was succeeding. I was making friends, passing the exams I'd failed before. I was accepting my new reality.

And I felt now there was no limit that I couldn't surpass.

Once at home, doing my homework in my room and studying for the final exam the next day, I looked at the helicopter with different eyes. I seemed to see a light, two of them, on one piece of the nose and another in the blades. It could be that . . .

But just then something leaped onto my lap. Despite our cat having lived with us for a few years, I startled as if it were the first time. Mimine settled on my legs as if they were her rightful bed. She turned around twice, with her paws trembling to get used to the irregular surface, and lay down. It wasn't even two seconds before I started to pet her and fawn over her. It seemed like just yesterday when we found her.

This one weekend I had kept hearing sounds, like tiny gasps, right near the headboard of my bed. It was so strange that at first I started thinking seriously it was some evil spirit. That was the only explanation. That wall didn't go to any other room of the house but instead the exterior, a wall of cement and bricks built to withstand the elements. But what my room did have was a door to a small balcony that turned and continued beyond the corner.

It was impossible to access that part of the house from outside unless you were Spider-Man. While it might not seem logical, I almost believed in ghosts more easily than in an arachnid superhero.

Lacking any logical explanations, I went down to let my parents know.

"I'm hearing strange noises."

The three of us went out onto the balcony and turned the corner, after which came the empty stretch behind my wall, and we found two kittens trying to protect themselves from the cold, huddled against each other. We gawked at them, enthralled. They were the most adorable things we'd ever seen. I took a step forward to pet them, but right when

I bent down, and even before I could beg my parents that we had to keep them, Mamá stopped me.

"We can't touch them, or we'll contaminate them with our scent and their mother won't want them."

"But they're all alone. They seem abandoned," I said, stating the obvious. "Can't we keep them?"

Papá laughed, of course. Both of them had been waiting for that question, and I was dying to ask it.

"Your mother's right," he said. "Don't you see how tiny they are? They can't even open their little eyes."

"How long can they have been here?"

"It looks," Mamá intervened, "like their mother has just fed them and left to go hunt for herself."

"Will she come back?" I couldn't say why, but I had the feeling those kittens were completely abandoned, that their mother wouldn't return.

"Of course she will. That's why you can't touch the kittens; otherwise the mother will get confused. She'll think they're not hers, and she'll abandon them."

We went inside only to discover, the next day, the mother had done both things: she'd taken one of her offspring and abandoned the other, a female kitten with black-and-white fur who wouldn't stop whining and mewling as if her life depended on it.

Which it did.

We couldn't leave her out there, alone and abandoned. Only once we'd confirmed the mother wasn't coming back for her did we pick her up and bring her inside from the balcony to spend the night somewhere warm and comfortable. On lifting her, her meows increased in intensity. She was frightened and thought we were going to hurt her. But once we'd wrapped her in some tiny blankets and given her a bit of milk with a bottle, the kitten calmed down and fell fast asleep. She was exhausted.

While she rested, we decided among all of us what to do with the little thing. First we'd have to bring her to the vet to make sure she was healthy. Then we'd get information about how we could put her up for adoption. We'd look for a family who would love her and could take care of her.

"But we could take care of her," I protested.

It wasn't any secret how much I liked animals. In fact we'd had various pets at home, like my hamster, Rémy. It was natural for me to insist we keep her. It couldn't hurt to ask.

"Yes, please, Mami, please, Papi, let's keep her. Please, porfa!" Naia begged.

"There are already so many of us in this household," they offered as an excuse to avoid saying something even more absurd to justify it.

Their protests didn't even last two days. After the veterinarian's tests, the cat was already more part of the family than any of us. She followed us, cooed at our feet, played with us without fear. And the farce of trying to give her up for adoption faded into oblivion as soon as we started to call her Mimine. She was ours already. We'd given her affection and love. We'd loved her without caring about anything more. If her mother had come back, Mimine wouldn't have cared, because she already had a true home with us.

Caressing her that afternoon, I remembered all that. How frightened she was during those first few days and how comfortable she felt later, clawing the sofa, discovering all the corners of the house. From a squalid and trembling kitten, she turned into a healthy and playful cat, one who knew no fear and leaped from furniture to furniture. We'd given her love and a belief in herself.

That was when I realized what was truly going on with me and gave a name to that feeling inside my chest. I felt confidence, stability. After having spent months locked inside myself, I opened and let light in. Suddenly everything began to flow. The love of those around me, the effort I spent in studying, the friendship my classmates offered me . . . Everything added up. Nothing was left over.

And every piece fit.

Finally.

Something led me to suddenly leap up from the bed to reach for the LEGO helicopter on my shelf. Mimine also leaped quickly from my lap, jumping onto the desk and curling up on top of my half-finished homework. She seemed to tell me I had something more important to do. I went back to the bed and, with my legs crossed, placed the toy in front of me. Its days as a helicopter were numbered.

There before me, without knowing it, I had what would be the future MK-1.

The moment had arrived.

CONNECTIONS
AND GOALS

They were days of intense work. I lived only for building that project, which, without my knowing it, would change my life forever.

"David," Mamá called from the other side of my door. As I tried to fit some pieces together, sweat slowly dripped across my forehead. I knew two things very clearly at that moment: that a design could work really well in theory but not in practice, and that my parents turned on the heating too early. It was only the end of October, but needless to say it wasn't cold enough to need it yet. "Are you going to have dinner with . . . ?"

A click alerted me that she was trying to open the door.

"Don't come in!" I implored, almost shouting.

The door pulled shut, and I heard the click of the doorknob closing once more and *"d'accord, d'accord"* repeated a few times.

"I was just asking if you're going to have dinner with us or up here."

I could tell she was clearly exasperated.

"Up here, please." I heard her sigh even from the other side of the door. "But you don't need to bring it up, OK? I'll come down when I can."

"It'll get cold."

This time I was the one to sigh. I knew she said it for my own good, but in my head, at just eighteen years old, after so many months in a well that was too deep, too dark, and maybe somewhat unsalvageable but not impossible to overcome, at last I had something that motivated me: the future MK-1. And now there was no dinner that could drag me away from the construction I had delayed working on for so long.

"I'll heat it in the microwave, don't worry. Really."

"*Comme tu veux, chéri!* But your days of staying locked in there will come to an end," she warned. She didn't know it, but her words were about to become reality.

The arm was almost ready and had taken me only a few days of complete isolation. Well, not really complete.

I'd just reduced all my activities to the barest minimum. When I got out of school, I went straight to my mother's travel agency to do my homework as quickly as possible, so I could continue devoting myself to my project as soon as I got home. I did everything I could to spend as many hours as possible in the house—just the opposite of what an ordinary guy my age would do. After school, I ran up to my room and started to put together pieces, and as I held them against my arm, with the help of a fabric strap, ideas would start to fly.

Trial and error was my creed, and as many ideas sprouted in my mind as there are colors and shapes of LEGO, forcing me to reconsider the entire assemblage if I found myself with any difficulty. Little by little it was less that dusty yellow LEGO helicopter and more the arm it still was yet to be.

Therefore, to gain more time, I begged my mother to let me have dinner in my room, and we had conversations like the one mentioned above almost every night. On the nights when she did bring my dinner upstairs, I poked my head out the door, grabbed the plate, and didn't let her come in or even let her get a peek through the half-open door.

Only my father managed to steal a snapshot. It had to be him, of course, the one who had always recorded me on video and had taken thousands of photos of me to have a historic register of my experiences. As if he knew fate had big surprises in store for me. The first night I didn't want to eat with all of them he already suspected something was happening and, knowing me, took advantage while electronic songs I'd composed myself were playing full blast to open the door slowly and stealthily and take a photo of me, one which he calls "The Photo," in which I have the strap around my arm, holding in place the first pieces of LEGO.

"*¡Madre mía!*" I shouted when I realized he was spying on me.

He dashed away with his characteristic little laugh, and I heard my mother, who was at the foot of the stairs, read him the riot act.

"What are you doing? What have you done? Leave him alone!"

"Look, take a look. I took a photo. Let's see it together."

Amazed by the photo, they guessed what I was trying to do and decided not to bother me anymore, leaving me to the task of creating something big, always proud of me.

I think that was why they proved so permissive in terms of my dinner habits. Surely . . .

But for me it was still a secret.

A surprise.

A colossal project. My grand project.

The pieces of the dismantled LEGO helicopter on my bed and a fabric strap to hold them in place around my arm were the beginnings of my grand project. Those pieces would come to have another life, another use, another identity. I started the arm one Monday and finished it on a Friday night.

Carefully, I placed my little hand (that's what we all called it at home) inside the construction, taking care that my *muñón* fit into the slots that, connected to the cables of some old headphones, would let me open and close the hand made from pincers. Then I turned a screw that tightened the lower part of the construction around my arm. Through an interior piston, I adjusted the prosthetic to the shape of my *muñón*, the mechanism keeping it together so it wouldn't fall off.

My heart beat so strongly I thought my chest couldn't take it. Can the beats of strong emotion break the sternum and propel all your feelings beyond yourself?

I made a few trials with the arm, and during one of them, it seemed like my chest was being put to the test, not the arm.

The headphones fulfilled their role as tendons, activating to open the pincers that served as my hand when I lowered the arm and close them when I raised it.

Yes, it worked. I was dying to show it to my parents, for them to see that I was OK, that little by little we'd emerge from this.

I felt unstoppable. I wanted to rush down to the living room so they could see it. But I remained rooted in place, agog, staring at it. It was perfect. The red and yellow pieces shone beneath the light of my desk lamp. I sighed and dried the sweat from my forehead. Dang heating! I had been so focused, leaning over the arm and under the lamp's spotlight, that I'd sweated over even the arm's last finishing touches.

I made my final checks. I slowly slid my arm into the apparatus I had created, as if I was afraid of it, and I could finally confirm that my *muñón*'s protuberances and shapes, which I used like tiny fingers, each fit perfectly into their anchors. The arm, which I'd just finished holding in place so it didn't slide, had two pieces held together with a screw and piston.

Just as I thought, everything was in order. The LEGO arm remained held to my flesh-and-bone arm, and the primitive hand at the end (three longish beams that functioned like a pincer and emulated the principal structure of a hand) opened and closed correctly with the movement of my *muñón*—what I call my *"codoñeca"* or "elbow-rist." Although it sounds sophisticated, the mechanism was really rather simple. Using the protuberances of my *muñón*, which I can move perfectly, I tensed and pulled on some headphone cables that stretched toward each end of the LEGO structure, which in turn were connected from the elbow to the pincer that served as a hand. That's how I opened and closed it.

Once I was sure my invention wouldn't fail, I got up from the desk, wearing the LEGO arm, and looked at myself in the mirror. For a second I couldn't breathe. It wasn't realistic. It didn't look normal (that's to say it didn't fit with the usual definition of "normal"). It was a LEGO enchantment that made me symmetrical and helped me feel the incredible sensation of picking up objects from a distance.

Before going down to the living room, I moved around in front of the mirror, acting as if I had two real arms. I raised my right hand to greet my own reflection, I stretched as if I were yawning, I shook both arms as if I were at a dubstep concert doing the wave with the rest of the audience or as if I were on a desert island trying to catch the attention of the tiny passenger plane crossing the sky above my head.

Never had I ever seemed to have such a vast sky above me, so large, so broad, and so infinite.

I couldn't hold back any longer, and I ran out of my bedroom. I'm sure that, on hearing the door and my hurried steps trotting down the stairs, my parents thought I was coming down at last for my missed dinner. I could have done that—the truth is I was starving, although I didn't realize. My emotions kept me from hearing the growls of my empty stomach.

As I went down the stairs, when I had almost reached the dining room, I said, "Papá, Mamá, turn off the TV. I want to show you something."

"David, it's very late," my mother protested when I arrived.

They were in the dark, watching a movie on TV, and I woke my mother, who was almost asleep. So they wouldn't see me, I hid my right arm behind my back. In those shadows they could barely see if my arm ended where it was supposed to end or if it kept going in a rush of red and yellow.

"Your mother's right. You shouldn't eat at this hour," my father continued.

"But—"

"You can't go on like this," Mamá interrupted me. "This business of locking yourself in your room without telling us what you're doing can't go on if it's going to affect your schedule. And if your grades suffer."

Well, for someone who was half-asleep, she seemed to suddenly be quite lucid.

"Don't be so hard, Nathalie. He went too far today, but I'm sure he's working on something that'll knock our socks off."

"I don't know," I said in a firm voice. This was no time for them to be yelling at me! "Why don't you two tell me?"

Despite the fact that using such a tone might have earned me a scolding at another moment, my parents turned their heads toward me, as if spring operated, without saying anything more. I merely turned on one of the lamps nearby and brought the LEGO prosthetic out from behind my back, letting it shine for itself.

Their reaction was immediate.

My mother raised her hands to her face, unable to believe what she was seeing.

Papá rose up as if the sofa had caught on fire, coming to startle Mimine, who ran across the living room and out of there. He approached me while Mamá stood up to better see what I had done.

"David, this—" she began.

"You did this?" my father finished, his eyes damp with emotion. "With LEGO pieces?"

He almost lost his voice with those words. To give you an idea, a rooster's crow at six in the morning is not stronger than the sound that escaped his throat at that moment.

I could do nothing more than offer a really huge smile while I nodded my head.

"It's much better than the one you made when you were nine."

"It seems almost real," Mamá stuttered. "It seems almost—"

"Almost professional," my father finished.

I laughed and begged them not to exaggerate, but they were too impressed. I realized it was hard for them to get a grip on what they were seeing; that was evident. After all those months of self-isolation, long faces, and failed exams, seeing their son take flight once more, seeing he'd emerged from the ashes, moved them. What shone in their eyes wasn't the reflection of the light from the TV or the lamp.

And I hadn't even shown them what it could do yet.

"Wait." I stopped them before they reached me. "There's more."

I approached the side table and with the LEGO arm grabbed the water bottle sitting on top of it. I opened the pincers with the little fingers of my *muñón*, closed them around the bottle, and, when it was held firmly in place, lifted it and brought it toward me. With my left hand, I removed the cap, and with the LEGO arm I raised the bottle to my lips and drank.

Out of the corner of my eyes I could see my father didn't miss a single detail and that his eyes were growing even more watery.

I also saw my mother was in danger of dislocating her jaw, it was hanging so low.

I was only drinking water—a normal gesture, right? But for the first time in eighteen years, since the first prosthetic, I did it with two hands. Yes, I was drinking water with an arm I had built from scratch with LEGO Technic pieces. After years of pitying looks and *penasco*, of breaking necks and putting up with kids who bullied me, and some girl or other who broke my heart, a gesture as simple as that—thanks to a mechanical arm—turned into a feat on the level of the Sistine Chapel or the Tower of Pisa (but without leaning).

Skillfully, I closed the bottle and set it down on the table. Mamá gave a few claps of joy, while Papá remained incredulous, his eyes shining, incandescent. I was encouraged to do something more, even though it wasn't planned. "And that's not all," I said without ceasing to smile.

I bent down and stretched out on the floor facedown. I put both hands in position, under my chest, and pressed the tips of my toes against the ground to raise myself up with the help of the muscles of my arm and the LEGO structure. I did some push-ups like this. Just two. Not because I couldn't do more (at that moment I felt capable of doing anything, of running all the way around the world without stopping, of brushing the moon if I leaped) but because I didn't want to stress the structure's mechanism.

When I got up, my mother threw herself on me in a hug that left me without any air. She babbled that she couldn't believe it, that it was marvelous, that my little head was full of crazy ideas, and that the arm was impressive. That what I had done was something incredible, and that what had happened when I was nine was just the start of my story.

My father, for his part, just stared at me with his damp eyes, and a tear of pride slid down his cheek. He came toward me, drying the tear that had escaped, and put one hand on my right shoulder. I could tell how happy he was, how surprised I'd left him, how proud he felt of me at that moment, as he always was with everything I managed to do for myself.

I felt happy seeing my parents so amazed and proud that I had managed to build the great project of my life with my favorite toy.

"David," Papá said, "if you fall because of your arm, I'll use your arm to lift you up."

And then, for the first time in my life, I could hug my father with two arms.

None of us could imagine how much our lives would change after that night.

WELCOME, MR. LEGO

What should the next step be? Anyone finding themself in this situation would ask that question.

Do you all see? David Aguilar, the boy who is six fingers away from his eleventh, finally had a right arm. It was a brand-new, fire-red-and-golden-yellow robotic-looking LEGO Technic arm that made him look like the Andorran Terminator who had had to repeat the second year of *bachillerato*.

I looked at myself in the mirror and felt like a tough guy. My left arm finally had a companion, and I learned the true meaning of symmetry on my body. It was so strange to see myself like that. I, who had never wanted a prosthetic, found myself with that hunk of one I'd built myself, without the help of anyone, hanging from my arm.

But looking at myself in the mirror, I realized I didn't need it at all.

That LEGO arm could do things for me, of course. I tried everything: opening doors and closing them, doing push-ups, picking up objects, hugging, shaking hands (clumsily—I'd have to make some adjustments), riding a bike (my dad's, without any extensions), playing the guitar (it didn't work very well; the hand as I'd built it couldn't hold the pick properly). I even ventured to try my sister's jump rope.

Even so, I decided I didn't *need* it.

After all the exercises I practiced that Sunday, I took off the prosthetic and carefully examined my reflection once more, just as I'd done a few minutes earlier. I had the feeling that all my life had consisted of just that, an eternal contemplation before the mirror, ever since I'd looked at my reflection in the glass door on my first day of school until this very moment in my bedroom. For some people, the first thing they see are those extra love handles; others see acne on their face; a few are foolishly worried about having laughed too much and getting wrinkles. I always turned my gaze toward my arm. It was a reality. It was missing. And no matter how much I struggled to live a normal life, everything in my universe always wound up revolving around that absence. My *muñón* had its own gravitational force and attracted all gazes. Even mine.

I'd always understood clearly that this is how I was; that's it. I broke necks, I could tie my shoes with one hand, I could construct the little figures from the chocolate eggs in record time, I faced down the bullies who tried to mess with me, I frightened the kids from other schools when we went on trips, and I ducked snowballs as if I were in *The Matrix*. All with just one arm.

And that was enough.

I didn't need anything more. I didn't need any prosthetic, whether an orthopedic one or a LEGO one. Because this was me, a boy with five fingers on one hand and a *muñón*. I was David, and if something defined me, it wasn't my arm but my passion for LEGOs, building, inventing new projects, and creating them from scratch.

The MK-1, as I now called it, was born from my eagerness to embark on a new challenge, to surpass myself and live. In this final instance, it resolved a real mobility need. Alone, making my room into a shipyard, I had been able to build a ship (that was the prosthetic) without knowing it would carry me to destinations that before I had only dared to imagine in my wildest, craziest dreams. As the song my dad composed goes: *Y todo empezó con un barco que un buen día sus velas izó, y de la deriva me salvó. LEGO, a tierra firme me llevó.* (And it all began with a ship that one day raised its sails and saved me from drifting. LEGO carried me to solid ground.)

I knew it clearly: my body didn't need the prosthetic, but I boarded that ship and pulled up the anchors, because I'd started to think perhaps others did need it.

Could I come to help people like me? I'd built an arm for myself. Would I be able to build other arms? The lights and sounds I always saw and heard when I created things appeared again before me. Unexpectedly I saw how I could improve the MK-1 and convert it into a future MK-2. I began to think, just as Peggy had helped me and my whole family with that tiny gesture of tying her shoes, I could help that little kid who didn't know who he looked like, who thought he was alone, strange, a monster. I just needed to learn more anatomy and engineering, practice more, get my message out there, and . . . well, I didn't know anything more back then. What could I study to pursue these goals? How could I increase my knowledge at university? Would I need to study biology? Or would my path lie in engineering?

It was very early to think of all that. The school year had practically just begun. November entered our lives with cold, and I had managed to pass the first exams. This time everything pointed toward me earning my *bachillerato* degree, so it was time for me to think more seriously about university. The year before, with the cascade of events that had derailed me, I'd barely thought of my future aside from when I saw it as black as my mood. This time everything was different. Someone up there had extended a LEGO hand to me, and I liked to think it had been my *abuela* Basi. Seeing me with that prosthetic would have knocked her for a loop.

"David," my father said then, "this thing you've done is huge. You can't imagine how big it is, *cariño*. You left us speechless with the prosthetic you made when you were nine, but now . . . Your genius will be a great example for the world, don't you think? You could someday inspire millions of people all over the world."

He was excited. And not just that, he infected me with his enthusiasm. Could he be right? That might be good for the world but above all for me. For my self-esteem and confidence. For my mother, who had bought me so many LEGO sets over the course of my life. For my father, whose first encounter with disability was the day he saw me for the first time. I could help families who faced situations like the ones I had experienced. A world of possibilities opened before us.

You have an idea already of how clever my father is, but that night he outdid himself. Looking admiringly at my prosthetic, he said, "We need to make a video, David, but it's going to be overwhelming. Are you ready?"

"A video?" I replied, incredulous. "Wait, wait. Ready for what?"

"To change the world, to change how people see people like you. If we tell your story in a video, perhaps you could come to create a better world, one that's more humane and inclusive, one with more solidarity."

"Wow! But we're not going to make some superproduction, right?"

"No, just a simple, concise video. You introduce yourself, show the prosthetic, explain how you made it and how it works. And most of all explain what LEGO has meant in your life and how important it's been in your development. Then I'll edit it. You know I'm good at that."

I blushed, remembering the video he made for my eighteenth birthday party. It was incredible and the most emotional moment of the celebration.

"Then we'll post it on social media, tagging LEGO," he continued. "I'm sure the people at LEGO will be thrilled to see what you've managed to do with their pieces. Just think that behind each piece of your arm there are thousands of LEGO workers who you'll give yet another reason to see the dreams of children become reality thanks to their efforts. That will be the litmus test, what will give us the sign that your message and your story of struggle and triumph can go further."

"But do you think they'll see it?"

"I'm sure of it."

"I don't know, because they must be very busy there in Denmark with their bricks and things in LEGOLAND. Remember what an awesome theme park it is! Keeping that up takes time," I joked.

My father chuckled. Of course he remembered; he remembered very well. When I was little, my parents took me to Billund, Denmark, by surprise to visit the enormous LEGOLAND theme park. It was hard for them to bring me to an airport without my realizing it, and if they blindfolded me, someone in the security department might think I was being kidnapped. So my parents opted for an infallible technique: tricking their own kid. They told me we were going to Ibiza. I should have suspected something when they put thick sweaters in our suitcases instead of bathing suits and even when at the airport my father tried to block all the screens with his body and let me play with the Game Boy more than usual so I wouldn't lift my head to the screens announcing our flight. But the best of all was when, in the taxi on the way to the hotel, I saw an enormous billboard for LEGOLAND, and everyone pretended I had imagined it. They were so convincing I actually believed them! After all that, arriving at the park was a real surprise, and it was one of the best trips of my life. I cried from emotion at the very gates of the park. And of course that moment was also immortalized by Papá's camera.

"Whether or not they see it," my father concluded, "I think, at a minimum, we owe them this small homage. If on top of that they do see it and learn about your story, that's icing on the cake. Besides, this way the whole family and all our friends will know. It's going to blow their minds!"

We recorded the video that same afternoon. It was lots of fun explaining how I'd built the arm and how it worked. I felt like a university professor or a doctor who had just created some revolutionary invention.

David Aguilar presents . . . the MK-1, the revolutionary orthopedic from LEGO! I'm greeted with a standing ovation as I appear, dressed in a black turtleneck sweater, with the right sleeve rolled up all the way to my shoulder. I greet the audience, and when I reach the center of the stage, a spotlight illuminates a glass side table on which the prosthetic rests. I pick up the LEGO arm and put it on. Then I reveal all its secrets to the audience.

Well, the truth is the video was much simpler, homemade, and recorded in my bedroom, with my favorite LEGO constructions as the background. My father made it dynamic with transitions and sound effects that added the perfect personal touch.

Once it was ready, Papá uploaded it to Facebook, and as promised, he tagged LEGO.

"Now what?" I asked in his office, staring over his shoulder at the computer screen.

He turned in his chair and, as if it were the most natural thing in the world, shrugged his shoulders and said, "We wait."

That's how simple it was for him. I wondered when I'd attain that level of calm, that patience that seemed typical of adulthood, of parents, of grown-ups. Were they truly not impatient? How did they hide it so well? For my part I couldn't stop asking him every day if the people from LEGO had answered, if they have even shared the video on their own page (what a crazy idea!), and every day he answered no quite calmly, with a smile and a shrug of his shoulders.

However, he did share with me the reactions of all the people who had seen it: his colleagues at the bank, our relatives who didn't live in the city, friends of the family. Even Dr. Doncel and her daughter called to congratulate us. It seemed incredible to them.

But from LEGO, nothing! Even so my father seemed unconcerned. My expectations had skyrocketed with his enthusiasm to record the video, and now it seemed like he didn't even care. Who could understand my dad?

Without a doubt he knew how to hide it really well.

Months later he told me how nervous he'd been during those days, how he'd expectantly checked Facebook all the time on his cell phone to see whether there was any news from LEGO. He couldn't express in words his yearning for there to be some response, how he was moved thinking the company that had made me so happy—from that first LEGO City set with planes. I had managed to accomplish so much thanks to them. LEGO toys allowed my imagination to fly and reinvent their products (the instructions weren't just a guide and a path to follow; they were a point of departure, and the goal was a new beginning).

One day in the bar where my father always ate with his work friends, a client and friend of the team, Salvador, noticed him and said hello.

"Hey, guys, *¡buen provecho!*"

Papá raised his eyes from his phone and returned the greeting.

"Ferran, I've seen the video of your kid with the LEGO arm. What a marvel! He built that thing all by himself?"

His mouth full of salad, my father just nodded energetically.

"Wow, what a head he's got on his shoulders. Has LEGO said anything?" he asked interestedly.

"Not yet," my father replied with a grimace after swallowing. "But surely it won't be much longer. Although they must get so many notifications, perhaps our video will get overlooked."

"Impossible! A feat like this can't be overlooked. You've got half of Andorra amazed!"

My father thanked Salvador and checked his phone again. A red dot signaled a new notification. He clicked it without much expectation, thinking it must be from some neighbor. That made his surprise even greater. His heart skipped a beat, and he couldn't breathe.

> Ferran, you've left us speechless.
> David's strength and perseverance
> are the things that make us feel proud
> and the reasons why we want to keep
> creating opportunities for all the kids in
> the world to access our LEGO bricks.
> Many thanks for sharing this with us.
> An ENORMOUS hug from your LEGO
> family. (smiley).

LEGO had responded to our video. They congratulated me. They applauded my yearning to surpass myself, my love for their toys.

My father raised his hand to his mouth, bursting with emotion.

We still didn't know it, but that was just the beginning of everything.

FROM THE STARS

One day I woke up in a hotel 5,179 miles from home.
But I didn't realize it just then.

That's why I rolled over once more in bed, in the wrong direction, and ended up falling to the floor.

"Ay!"

I almost cracked my head open on the corner of one of the night tables.

The truth is I haven't discovered a better alarm clock than falling out of bed. It wakes you up like there's no tomorrow. (Although I could have done without the bruise on my arm.)

In the shower I looked more closely at the bruise. It was yellowish, but I could already see how purple it was going to get and how big it would grow. I couldn't help sighing.

Bruises, blows, falls. I couldn't believe I'd arrived *here*. This was the real deal.

Here was Houston.

It's hard for me to say it; it's hard to even *think* it. Not even I could believe it—I was at NASA.

Although I almost missed it by just this much. You won't believe it!

Twenty-four hours before that fall, I realized I'd made a mistake when I looked at the ticket. I admit it, I hadn't seen it in time. My father called me because my mentor at NASA and now good friend, Dmitris Bountolos, had gotten in touch with him, concerned to know where I was.

"What do you mean you made a mistake?" my father asked me over the phone, still sleepy because they'd just woken him. I had just asked him to come back to the airport and pick me up, but he seemed to focus on other subjects. Specifically, what did I mean I'd made a mistake, and how was it possible for me to make such a mistake. "You made a mistake? Did you get the time wrong?"

"No, no . . . The time is right."

"So then?"

"It's the day."

"What?"

"I got the day wrong."

"What?"

"Three a.m. on the fifth is not the 3:00 a.m. that's coming up but 3:00 a.m. yesterday."

There was a long silence on the other end of the line. I admit at this point I almost cracked up laughing. I don't know whether because of nerves or because of confirming aloud I'd gotten the date wrong in catching a transatlantic flight that would lead to my living out one of my biggest dreams, one of my craziest and unthinkable fantasies that had been coming true over the past few months.

"Don't worry, there's no reason to pick you up."

"You're going to leave me living in the airport like in that Tom Hanks movie?" I interrupted him.

"You should be in Houston in twelve hours, and you're going to be in Houston in twelve hours. I'm going to see if some other flight takes off in the next few hours, and I'll buy you a last-minute ticket."

"But it'll cost an arm and a leg."

"Doesn't matter. I've got a son who I'm sure will be willing to give one up." From the sound of his voice in my headphones, I could almost see him winking at me.

Soon after I had new tickets, and a few hours later, I embarked on a flight headed to the United States.

Once I reached the hotel, I collapsed.

In my dreams my father's phone was still ringing with Dmitris from NASA calling to ask where I was, saying they'd been waiting for me for hours. But Papá had already explained to them what had happened to me and that there was no problem. The only downside was I'd miss the guided tour at the hands of the chief of innovation himself, now also my good friend, Omar Hatamleh. What an introduction I'd made in front of a bunch of the directors of the most important companies in the world!

After showering that morning, I did laugh at how foolish I'd been to get the date wrong.

Be especially alert if you have to travel in the early hours, and think really hard about what day you need to catch your flight. I've left you speechless, haven't I?

What's important is I managed to arrive in Houston a few hours before my talk at the NASA Cross Industry Innovation Summit of Technology, where I'd been invited to present the prosthetics I'd built by then and speak of future projects I was working on. In my computer I carried one of the secrets reserved for the attendees of the event: the 3D design of my MK-5, built and conceived with the new LEGO Education pieces called SPIKE Prime that are going to revolutionize teaching. This time my invention had sensors and a programable switchboard. I was convinced they'd like the surprise, but . . .

Without that first prosthetic, nothing that day would have been possible. I had traveled down a long road before being able to arrive here.

That video of my MK-1 flew throughout the entire city. Friends of my father, my parents' colleagues, neighbors, teachers at school, classmates, my childhood buddies—all of them were fascinated by the perseverance I displayed in the construction of the splendid MK-1.

I took their admiration as well as I could. I was thrilled and excited, but at the same time I withdrew and wasn't sure how to react. Although it wasn't hard for me to be daring among my friends, I've always been shy when accepting this kind of praise and recognition. And this, after all, had to do with my arm, or its absence. You can find out in a moment like this whether you're the kind of person who sees the glass half-full or half-empty.

I've always been noticeable because of my *bracito*. People have always pointed me out because of it, and I've received "special" treatment, as if I am weaker than the rest: an invalid, a cripple, a poor *manco*! But now, instead of seeing it as a lack or a defect, they saw it as something positive and advantageous, like a unique and different characteristic.

They saw it, at last, through my eyes.

I realized then that all those necks that had broken had not been in vain, that when I gave back to people, they had opened and learned from the "books" they expected me to carry in my backpack. Over time they had seen as clearly as I did that my left arm wasn't a lack or an absence or an equation to resolve: the X was solved from the first day, because I was a complete person.

Now, when they walked by me, nobody turned around in surprise to count how many extremities I had. Now they greeted me and offered me a high five. And what faces they made when I raised my *muñón*, but then I laughed and raised my other hand, and the smack sounded ecstatic, thrilling.

What I lived during those days was inexplicable, because suddenly I found myself with the recognition I had always, somehow, wished to get from others. I had always wanted them to see me the same as I did, through my eyes, to understand my experience, realize I wasn't a cripple, wasn't useless. If that proved to still be so important to me at this stage, how might my life have been if I'd had people's understanding and recognition much sooner?

When the first journalist wanted to tell my story, I knew what they had to do: they had to reach that three-year-old David looking at himself in the glass door of school and, no matter how hard he looked and observed and searched, not finding himself. They had to reach the nine-year-old David who didn't stop examining himself in the mirror and whose gaze always went to the same place, the same absence. They had to reach the eleven-year-old David who suffered consciously for that deformity people had always attributed to him. The MK-1 had ceased to be a nebulous project in my head and a construction made of LEGO pieces, and it had turned into a message with which to inspire thousands of kids.

I could create change. I could put an end to the stigma against disability. I could offer my grain of sand to mitigate bullying and help the kids who suffer from it feel supported, that they weren't alone.

Because all of us are different, but none of us is incomplete.

THE CLICK

When Papá saw LEGO's reply (I didn't learn this until much later), he not only felt swollen with pride and overwhelmed with emotion but also thought of me. Of all I had suffered. Of my first day of school, when I was searching like crazy for someone like me and how the only consolation I found was in my own reflection. When I got knocked over and we thought I'd injured my coccyx. When I had to defend myself with real blows against snowballs. When my heart was broken for being different.

He realized this could be the moment.

The moment to get up. The moment for me to see my own worth and what I was capable of.

To make me believe in my own dreams.

"Rosa?" my father said when he heard the other end of the line pick up. "It's Ferran. I need your help."

Rosa Alberch, a journalist for RTVA, Andorra's television station, had seen everything: LEGO's reply, the post my father wrote on his Facebook page about it, everyone's enthusiastic and affectionate responses to it. She was already amazed and moved, even before my father explained everything I'd had to go through. She admired what my father wanted to do for me and how I could become a symbol for so many kids like myself with a bit of help.

"Ferran, what you're doing for your son is incredible. Of course I'll help. Tomorrow we can go to school to record something for the program *La Rotonda*, if that works for you."

"I'll ask the director right away. They're also very enthusiastic at the school. They want David to give a speech to the ESO students! I can't believe it. It's . . ."

"Incredible," Rosa agreed.

I won't get into whether what I'd done was impressive. I think over all these pages you've been able to see I haven't been the best judge of myself. What is obvious is there aren't words or pages enough to describe or explain how I feel about everything my father has done and does for me. How much the help and support I've gotten from my mom and dad means to me. How much the overflowing love I've received from everyone means to me.

That call to Rosa Alberch, and the one to Albert Batalla, mayor of Seu d'Urgell, to ask for the phone number for Rosa Matas from the *La Vanguardia* newspaper, and calls to various other people were the start of a thrilling journey that would lead me from one newspaper to another, from one television station to another. The story of my arm, the LEGO bricks, and my passion for building things went around the world with headlines that introduced me as "Hand Solo," the nickname of my YouTube channel. I never thought I could come to be known like that, by that name, thanks to the channel I'd created to upload my covers of electronic music. I recorded them with a digital camera I placed above the keyboard so viewers saw only my left hand tapping the Launchpad. I got the name for the channel from that image, and that's where we also uploaded the video of my prosthetic. Now half the world knew me by that name, and the other half was starting to know me and my story. My story spread. From the *New York Times* to the *Washington Post*, from Reuters to Euronews, not to mention radio programs and even television channels from Japan, Russia, and China, to being one of the most watched videos on CNN.

Like us, all of them believed in the story we had to tell and the message we wanted to transmit.

Sometimes raising your own voice is not enough; it's not enough to shout until you're left without air in your lungs if you're doing it alone. You need people to support you, who raise their voice alongside yours and believe in your dreams. That's something I was never missing at any moment, starting with my own family. While I might not have a right arm, what I was never lacking was love.

On one of those days when the whirlwind of news and media seemed to have relaxed a little, Papá knocked at my door to tell me something even I could barely have imagined. Yes, there are still incredible moments left to tell you about, beyond even NASA or the LEGO Education program in Billund. Just wait a few pages.

I was studying in my bedroom. One might consider it early to begin studying for my final exams, but that year I wasn't going to leave anything to chance. I was ready to go to university and had just gotten an offer to study bioengineering at the International University of Catalunya (UIC). They'd requested that I come to give a conference there. How crazy was that? It was an option that appealed to me more and more.

Parents and teens attended the event in order to clarify the same doubts I had just then, to help decide what path to follow. There I was, in front of eight hundred people, just eighteen years old and responsible for my first speech. I took a deep breath and began, determined to explain my story and the functioning of my MK-1, which they had seen recently on Spanish national television on Javier Cárdenas's program *Hora Punta* (*Prime Time*). They knew me, but I wanted to surprise them—and a few days earlier I'd created my MK-2 based on a new jet plane. When I saw it parked on the shelves of the biggest shopping center in my country, Jordi Cachafeiro, its manager, gave the plane to me so I could fulfill my vision. He's a good friend of the family and soon after became the most important sponsor of the documentary about me.

Oh, sorry! I still haven't told you that a documentary movie of my story was made. Please have a bit more patience—I'll get there!

One of my passions is aviation, and ever since I was very little I've loved to build and invent my own creations. Maybe it's not so surprising that my first two arms sprang from a helicopter and a plane. It seems incredible that from a passion that lets your imagination soar (what a great image!) might arise ideas that let you touch the sky.

When I had Cachafeiro's gift safely home, I took it out of the box to build my new arm, which would be much better than the previous one. The undercarriage motor would give me the ability to pick up heavier objects, and its battery, placed at the biceps, could be activated through a piece tied to a shoelace that wrapped around my shoulder.

I'm sure it's easy to imagine what happened when I activated it in front of that group of parents and teens and the motorized noise put an end to their attentive silence. The hall erupted into a loud, surprised ovation, followed by a warm applause that enveloped me in this experience, which was changing my life.

That was how the UIC invited me to study within its classrooms.

Perhaps you're wondering what bioengineering is. Explained very simply, bioengineering is what comes closest to putting into practice my passion for making prosthetics. More and more I thought this was the path for me to follow. My parents were thrilled for me to pursue it, and together we looked for the best universities where I could follow those aspirations.

Although I'd already been considering it for some time, the final push was given to me by our friends Pere and Pilar.

My parents had always raised and educated me to show that I alone, without the help of anyone, was able to achieve everything I wanted to do. While I was doing just that (for the most part), I also felt the need to go beyond that and help others, especially people like me, have confidence in themselves and feel independent or autonomous or both. What I wanted was to share with everyone my way of seeing the world. Nothing more, nothing less.

"David, can I come in?" my father asked, poking his head through the doorway one evening during those months after the video went viral. Since I was taking a brief break, I let him come in. Both he and my mother always asked for my permission to interrupt my study sessions, and they did so only when they thought it was necessary. "You're not going to believe the proposal we've just gotten."

Those were very common words at that time, and the range of things he had to tell me was really broad: from a beloved local newspaper interested in my story to a national television program. But really, that time Papá was right. Because I was going to be in *National Geographic*.

I couldn't believe it.

Was my face, my arm, my non-forearm really going to appear in one of the most renowned scientific magazines of the world? Was I, David Aguilar, the star of that moment, or had I gotten confused about which body I lived in? That sensation would become common during those months and sometimes still is even today. It's complicated to be the protagonist when you've been only the narrator.

So you'll understand me, think of something incredible that's happened to you. Do you have it? Any moment will do, from your parents taking you to Disneyland by surprise to the person you really like kissing you for the first time to eating an ice cream and finding the wooden stick inside that meant you won the big prize to hitting that unbelievable grand slam in phys ed. In those moments you feel what's happening with such intensity it seems like you leave your own body and live the event as if you were a spectator. You've reproduced that film in your head so many times you know it by heart. You've aced the trials, and now your heart is overflowing with so much joy you can contemplate that episode of your life only from the outside.

That is called dissociation, and I think I didn't return to myself until we received the copies the editors sent us when the issue was published. The photos were taken by Pau Fabregat, and they were amazing! A true *National Geographic* photographer immortalized me and my prosthetic. My father says it's one of his greatest achievements at cold-calling.

He was absolutely sure my story would be of enormous scientific value, and one day he got the idea to share it with that esteemed magazine. We were on our way to a Spanish television program, and when we stopped for coffee, he took advantage of the moment to send a private message to the editors through Facebook. He wanted them to share his son's story of triumph, or *superación* as we say in Spanish.

And he managed to get it! My story touched their souls and woke their curiosity to learn more about me and especially about what I had achieved.

Although they told us they had already finished programming the contents for every issue for the following year, in January they reserved a spot for me in the April issue.

"Ingenuity, perseverance, and resilience," read the headline. They were the three foundations on which I had managed to construct the MK-1 and MK-2 and on which I would build the MK-3. When copies of the magazine arrived, I was thinking about it, the MK-3, in breaks from my studies. It would be based on an impressive yellow LEGO Technic crane. That specific model was perfect for my new project. With its pistons and mechanized pieces, the new prosthetic would be able to not just raise and lower the arm like previous ones but also bear greater weight. My passion for LEGO developed my ability to construct things, that instinct of sounds and lights I used to join piece to piece until I created something unexpected.

My story, in a top scientific magazine like *National Geographic*, began to reach people who really needed it.

With all the overwhelming love and support that had reached me since I'd gone viral, I couldn't help but remember with every day, and even every hour, my *abuela* Basilisa. More than a year had passed since she'd left us, and although I missed her affectionate caresses, embraces, kisses, and words (her voice had dissipated in my memory like the steam off a hot chocolate—sweet until the end, bitter when it's over), her love remained around us like a warm blanket.

Sometimes I felt she was the wind that guided my voice to others' ears. I was sure she'd have been so proud her heart wouldn't fit in her chest. She would have gone, I'm sure, throughout the neighborhood, boasting of her grandson, like any grandmother would have done. She'd be at the butcher, and the neighbor would ask about me, and she wouldn't stop talking for even a minute. She'd go to the beauty parlor and show the hairdresser a photo album with clippings from all the newspapers and magazines I'd appeared in, including the one that was most special for her, the one that would have made her shout out loud, leap with joy, and kiss the very page where my photograph appeared. By now you should know the one I mean: *Pronto*. That article would have made her happier than any other, for it was the magazine she always read, the one she liked most and that enlivened her idle moments. Suddenly her grandson, *"su niño,"* appeared in its pages.

I was thrilled myself when I saw that small piece printed among the magazine's pages. Just thinking of all she would have felt, how much she would have liked to see my achievements—the result of the efforts she knew so well—recognized by so many people and talked about by journalists, newscasters, and everyone . . . With that happy coincidence, I felt everything had found its place in the world, that everything fit. I thought, in reality, what are poorly called coincidences are actually pieces of life that have found their connection, as if we're all part of a master plan devised by some wildly mad brain—sometimes bizarre, but always lucky.

We keep a copy of that issue of *Pronto* as a souvenir, and the evening it was published we toasted in my *abuela*'s honor, for our life with her and for everything that still remains for us to live, with her memory always embracing us.

The coincidences didn't stop there—although, as I've already told you, I don't believe in them, because I know everything is connected. Sometime later I learned the journalist who wrote the article in *Pronto* under the pseudonym MM was Manuel Marín, father of a child with psychomotor retardation and developmental delays. Manuel is an outstanding person with an impressive sensitivity who didn't want my story to go unnoticed, and with his article he wanted to also pay an homage to his son Víctor and all the children and parents who live these experiences. All this I learned by chance after his wife, Maribel Espinosa, invited me to give a brief talk to a small group of students in the inclusive school Auró in Barcelona, which Víctor attends every day with an enthusiasm to learn and learn.

That was the first time I gave a talk in a school. It was a unique experience to explain my story and see the fascination in the faces of all those kids gawking at me as if I were Tony Stark himself. The joy and wonder of that extraordinary event organized by the school's director, the teachers, and the parents' association filled me with so much emotion. They wouldn't stop thanking me, but I was the one who should thank them. They made me feel like a true superhero.

If I wasn't already sure before, that experience helped convince me: I needed to keep sharing my story around the world.

Do you remember that moment in *Spider-Man* when Uncle Ben tells Peter Parker: "With great power comes great responsibility"?

Well, I felt like my prosthetic gave me a great power, so I had the responsibility of fighting against the stigma of disability and bullying in favor of greater inclusion and visibility. The true disability lies in believing you can't achieve anything, and I didn't want to leave my prosthetic in a box and ignore the great opportunity of being Hand Solo, another Avenger in the fight against evil.

With this in mind, the days and weeks kept passing with similar surprises. That mad engineer who planned the universe didn't tire of sticking me in situations to show me that nothing in this life happens by chance but just the opposite: everything that happened in my life seemed to be part of some plans that were sketched and reordered according to the decisions I made and built piece by piece, unstoppable.

"Hello?" I answered my mobile almost on the last ring, perplexed by the really long phone number I read on the screen.

As usual I was studying in my room, but I'd forgotten to silence my phone.

"*Bonjour.* I'm looking for David Aguilar. *C'est vous?*" I heard on the other line in French. I wondered whether to hang up, thinking it must be some phone operator trying to sell me a new service or wanting to chew my ear off so I would switch companies. Despite that, and without suspecting in the least how wrong I was, I answered that I was he. "Delighted to greet you," he continued. "Look, my name is Yannick Dupont, and I'm calling you from LEGO Education. We have a proposal for you."

THE FINAL PIECE

Y ou did what?" my father shouted when I told him.

To tell the truth, that was the *last* reaction I was expecting. I didn't think I'd done anything crazy; in fact, I'd been mature, prioritizing my studies. I couldn't get sidetracked now.

"I told them no."

My mother froze with her mouth hanging open, and my father took off his glasses and rubbed the spot between his eyes. The David of the future practically pulls out his hair when he remembers all this. Really, I didn't have any idea what I was doing.

"Do you have any idea what you've done?"

I nodded, still not understanding why it seemed so incredible to them, despite having explained my position.

"You've just turned down working with LEGO!"

"I know that! But I wasn't going to sign any contract, Papá! I'm just nineteen, and I've got to finish high school."

"But let's take a look at this, David. What contract did they talk about?" my father tried to reason.

"Are you sure it was a work contract?" my mother added, trying to untangle this mess I'd gotten myself into all on my own.

"Well, I don't know. I guess so. Are there other kinds of contracts?"

"We'll see. I'm sure we can call them and get to the bottom of everything. Do you remember what they told you?"

"That they were calling from LEGO Education, and they wanted to make me an offer . . ." I struggled to remember, as if the call had come a week ago and not just fifteen minutes earlier. "They'd seen my video and had been following my achievements in the news. But before telling me anything more, I had to sign a contract of . . . of . . ." I'd been so surprised by the call that I barely retained what they'd told me, not to mention my head was full of the subjects I'd been studying.

"Of confidentiality?" Papá asked.

"That's it!" I replied. "And I don't know, I thought it was better if I didn't sign anything, I've got to finish school and . . ."

I couldn't say anything more because my father broke down laughing. If earlier I had understood little, now I understood even less. But it was all cleared up soon enough. My father explained it would have no repercussions on my academic life or my plans for the future. LEGO Education only wanted to tell me, under a framework of confidentiality, about the project they wanted me to participate in.

"It's to avoid secrets leaking out," he continued, still laughing. "You know, so that you don't go shooting your mouth off because you're so happy to be working with them," he explained. "It's not binding at all to what you do, just to your silence. You sign it, they explain the project, then you decide if you want to take part or not."

There was a moment of silence. I stood there staring off into space as that—and the answer I'd given to LEGO—slowly sank in. Was it possible? Had I just . . . ?

"Did I just say no to LEGO?"

After absolutely everyone had asked again and again if LEGO had done anything for me, I'd rejected them! I couldn't have stuck my foot (or my arm) in it any further if I'd tried.

Luckily, my father was the one who'd given my phone number to Yannick during an earlier phone call. He'd been eating with some clients, Stephane and Daniel, when the phone rang. Yannick couldn't explain the motive of his call to my father; he could only explain it to me. Papá had warned Yannick already that depending on how things went with that call, he would intervene. And boy did he!

My father chose to laugh, because, in the end, it's always better to try to take the mistakes we make in life with a sense of humor.

◆ ◆ ◆

As I went up to the podium at the NASA Summit of Technology, I started to remember this whole episode— especially when one of the MKs I was carrying fell to the floor before I reached the stage. What an entrance! But I didn't freak out over it. I had to stay focused. I'd decided to show the other three and spend my time talking about my projects with LEGO Education right after presenting, exclusively for this audience, the MK-5, designed expressly for this event through a 3D design program. These things happen: you will stumble, and it will seem like everything is in danger and about to shatter, but what's important, and what people will remember, is that you know how to recover. And then no one pays any attention to the stumble.

That was exactly what I did, both at the NASA talk as well as when LEGO came knocking at my door. That very afternoon, we got in touch with LEGO Education

and cleared things up. Yannick couldn't help but chuckle
at the misunderstanding. What surprises me now is that he
managed to hold in so much laughter. I can't help laughing at myself when I think of it. We gave him our mailing
address, and the confidentiality contract arrived the next
day by urgent courier. Papá read it carefully (as one should
do with any contract) and, seeing that everything was cor-
rect, I signed it, and we sent it back right away.

"We want you to spend a week with us at LEGO
Education this summer," the head of the project explained.
"We'll show you our facilities, you'll take part in a project
where you'll attend some very special classes, and you'll give
talks to different work groups and managers who are eager
to meet you and your prosthetic. You'll develop a prosthetic with us, using our new pieces. You have tremendous
potential and unique creativity, and we think that, working together with us, you can do a lot for other kids like
yourself. What do you say?"

"Can I . . . ask something before I respond?"

"Of course, go ahead!"

"Can I meet the person who designed the helicopter I
made the MK-1 from? And the designer of the plane that
became my MK-2?"

(Don't judge me, I was living my childhood dream!)

Yannick, touched, couldn't help laughing.

"Of course! In fact, they're the same person, and they're dying to meet you and talk with you about how you built the prosthetic. You have no idea how much everyone is looking forward to meeting you at LEGO House!"

To say I'd been about to miss the chance of my lifetime because of some silly confusion would be an understatement. LEGO Education's proposal was much more than I could have dreamed, even guided by the persistence and perseverance that have marked me since I was little. What I found here before me was basically the pinnacle of what I'd hoped to reach since we had started to share my story. I was given the chance to offer my potential to people like me, people who needed an arm, who needed inspiration. During those months of media whirlwind, we were even contacted by talent programs, but my family and I didn't think my abilities lay in that direction. I didn't build replicas of great European monuments or scale models of iconic cities of the world. My constructions were meant to be used, not admired; they *wanted* to be useful. I didn't think they should be displayed unless it was for educational or scientific purposes. I wanted to help people, inspire them, motivate them, research how to make their lives better if they needed—and LEGO was offering me the chance to do so.

"Of course, count on me," I told them. "I'm thrilled to be able to work with you and develop my skills even more."

You have to believe me when I say I don't remember what happened after that phone call: whether I screamed out loud, if I jumped for joy, if I celebrated it in style with my family. All I see of the memory is the color yellow, the color of happiness and light for me, like when I learned to ride a bike.

The end of the school year came faster than I expected. Final exams and the selectivity test surrounded me like a tireless tornado that rattled all my pieces. But I endured and, now unbeatable, passed everything this time and won a place at college.

The golden moment of that summer, however, came when I boarded that flight to Denmark that would take me to the offices of LEGO Education.

There I did all the things they'd told me over the phone and much more. I spent hours imagining new prosthetics created exclusively with the new LEGO pieces, I learned from their engineers, I visited the facilities, I spoke in front of their board of directors. Yannick accompanied me at all times, and although he made me feel like I was at home, I was so immersed in the experience I felt like the synapses of my neurons had disappeared and become the connections of LEGO pieces. Yannick was my mentor in LEGO and the precursor to this whole journey of experiences and emotions. I am proud to be able to call him a friend and now even consider him to be a member of our family.

In those days, there was space in my head only for those prosthetics of the future, and the pulsing emotions I felt blocked me from thinking of anything beyond those prosthetics.

Thinking about those days still gives me the same feelings. In fact, in remembering them I still get so moved I can barely put it down in black and white. How can you describe the feeling of your dreams coming true? I could see the spaceships I'd built when I was little and their crews, little LEGO minifigures, greeting me and winking at me, saying, "Mission accomplished, David. Houston, we're coming home." I managed to touch the stars by climbing a LEGO ladder, put together piece by piece by myself.

If I was dizzy, wait until you see how my father felt.

"How'd it go? How'd it go?" he asked nonstop when I landed back in Barcelona.

It was my fault, really. Those days in Denmark were such complete craziness that I had no time to think of anything else. I called my family every few days so they didn't worry about me too much, but I told them barely anything. I was too eager to get back to the studio and the projects I was building. There would be time for talking later, and that moment came when I arrived home from the stay at LEGO Education. At the airport, as we walked through the parking lot toward the car, I explained to my father a thousand details, which he drank up eagerly. His eyes shone brightly, proud and half-incredulous of everything I told him, of the fact that I had reached this point in my life.

"Wait a minute . . . Do you know where we are?" I interrupted. It was the third time we'd passed in front of the same row of cars, and we'd changed levels at least twice. I stopped short and held him back.

"What silly questions you ask! We're in the parking lot," he replied, and kept walking while he talked. "Now, keep telling me what the engineer who showed you how . . ."

It was obvious he was trying to beat around the bush to avoid the subject, but the suitcases were too heavy to keep walking in circles!

"Papá, you've forgotten where you parked!"

"I did not! The car is right near here!"

"Near here? On the lower level, right?" I criticized. We were getting closer and closer to the elevator!

"David, the car is here . . . somewhere."

"I can't believe it," I said, laughing. I was practically giggling.

"Well, fine, *hijo*, I don't know where it is," he confessed. "But how do you expect me to remember? I got out of the car and ran to meet you because we've barely spoken in days. I was so nervous and also really eager for you to tell me everything you've done. So here we are. Looking for the car. We've already covered half the parking lot, so there isn't that much more."

In the end we did finally find the car, and on the way home we both cracked up over Papá's big mix-up. (It was in another building, not the one where we were searching!) That wasn't the only mistake of the summer. Those months were special, thrilling, unique. It wasn't just the stay at LEGO Education; it was also the beginning of my life as an adult, the end of high school, and going off to university.

I remember my graduation from *bachillerato* as if it were right now, as if I were seated in the auditorium of school, squeezed into a white shirt with the right sleeve rolled up, and wearing my most elegant pants. I was happy, shining with joy, first because I'd reached the end of the year. I'd managed to get my *bachillerato* and could now continue my studies. Second because of all the people I'd been able to meet thanks to repeating a year. All of them, without exception, had turned into a second family who supported me and shared with as much enthusiasm as I did myself all the achievements, interviews, and visits of TV reporters to the school occasioned by the MK-1 and later the MK-2. But without a doubt, none of that would have been possible without the support of my teachers, who even encouraged me to give talks to the ESO students about being bullied and how to succeed. All of them gave me the chance that afternoon at my graduation to talk in representation of my class. It was a speech none of us would forget.

Once more, I was going to give a big surprise to one of the people who had helped make possible the work of spreading my message around the world. A person who had let my school become my own Cape Canaveral, my center of operations from where my story would take off toward the stars with an incredible explosion. The place where a huge part of my life had taken place since I was little, and that, thanks to its director, Ana Villas, and all the staff who had taught me so much had made it possible for me to turn into the person I am today.

"And now David Aguilar would like to share a few words with all the students, parents, and teachers of this graduation of 2017."

That moment arrived after all my classmates had received their graduation degrees.

Once they were seated, I made my way through them and climbed, nervous but determined, to the stage of my school, located in the gym where I had lived through so many experiences and pranks. Among the audience I could see María, who had promised to come and see me and with whom I couldn't graduate the year before. Once I was up there, with the microphone in my hand and wearing that orange graduation sash, it was hard for me to start.

"I've grown up in the Colegio Sant Ermengol, and whenever I suffered any difficult moment, the teachers came to help me. Those moments are when you realize who loves you and who doesn't, but I had the great fortune of feeling loved by both them and my classmates. And it's not until you've lived that you realize how important it is. Today I stand before you to give all of you my thanks, because this school year has been incredible. I repeated second this year, and I admit I thought it would be horrible. But I was wrong, because I've lived unrepeatable moments with all of you. With the help and love I got, I managed to find the strength at the worst moment of my life to build my prosthetic, and you gave me your admiration for it. Who could have known that repeating a year would have given me time to make a LEGO prosthetic that would change my life?"

The audience broke into unexpected applause, and I could see among all the faces those of my parents, my sister, and my aunt Diana, with tears in their eyes.

"And thanks to it," I continued, "this school year, many TV stations have come to this school. I'd like to thank the director, Ana, for supporting me, because she always let the media come and record their programs. I'd like to give her a gift."

While everyone applauded, I addressed the extreme left of the stage, where Ana was, surprised by all of this. My accomplice, the director of studies, brought me a frame.

"What you see here is the article *National Geographic* devoted to me recently, which is the most important thing that has happened to me this year—aside from graduating from *bachillerato*! I want to give this copy that's framed and dedicated to our director, Ana Villas, as a gesture of thanks for everything." The audience broke into applause once more. "But I'd also like to dedicate this publication to each and every one of the teachers, tutors, and students of the Sant Ermengol school in Andorra la Vella who have stood by my side and accompanied me over the course of all these years. Your support has been necessary and essential for me to be the person I am today. All of you are my right arm, and you will always be a great part of me."

The audience stood up while Ana and I gave each other a warm hug.

After those final words, after the embrace, with a knot of emotion in my chest, I raised my gaze and stared ahead of me at a fixed point, because my future was there: I had decided to study bioengineering at the UIC, and nothing was going to stop me.

My father likes to say this was my *Wonder* moment. I had been so moved by that movie, which had made me cry at seeing myself reflected in it. I swear it's hard to make me cry! It's happened on only three occasions: when my grandmother passed away, after my heart was broken, and because of the compounded suffering of that boy I identified with so strongly. As of today it's still one of my favorite films.

Speaking in public is always tricky for me, whether it's in front of my classmates and friends, on local or national TV, or before the attendees of a conference at NASA. I can't help getting nervous, and I begin to sweat. I'm overwhelmed by a sudden feeling that I'm not doing things well. But as soon as I start to talk and remember why and for who I am doing all this, my doubts disappear, and there's just me, my voice, and my message: we are not alone and we are able.

No one knew yet that I had made my decision, but I was very clear about it. If my goal was to help people, my path lay in studying a degree that would help me do that.

The summer passed almost without my realizing it, between my nerves, preparations, and other celebrations. Without a doubt, one of the events that most surprised me was the congratulations I received on behalf of a centuries-old organization created by kings, noblemen, politicians, and artists on their granting me the silver medal of the Ligue Universelle du Bien Public for having done good for humanity. I was the youngest person who'd ever received it, and also with military honors. It was so incredible that to this day I find it hard to believe it happened. Was I really that kid in the grand salon of the État-major of the French Republican Guard, in the most emblematic building of Paris? Was that medal for me?

Life, as amazing as it was, had suddenly begun to seem unreal. But I had to start to think, and to *know*, that it was real, that my efforts, my persistence, my ability to push myself, and my skill for building things were bearing fruit. That effectively I had traveled a path without exhausting myself. And now was not the moment to stop but to go even faster.

"With this you can go everywhere, don't you think?" my father said, showing me the electric scooter he'd given me and adapted with prosthetic included. Homemade, of course!

"What is it?" I replied, incredulous.

"Well, it's quite a way from the dorm to the school building, and it'll be hard for you to park around there, no? We thought something like this would come in handy. What do you think? The prosthetic and the adaptation is Made in Ferran, like all the earlier ones." He winked at me.

I couldn't do anything but hug him. I loved the gift and tested that the prosthetic fit me perfectly, much better than the one on the bike, which was already starting to be too small for me again.

I began to feel as if I were truly about to take off, to run everywhere, and I noticed I was turning another page. One period was closing to give way to another once more.

That's what life should consist of, I told myself: periods that fit together, constructions that crumble only to leave space for a new building, one that's more solid, taller, and stronger. I knew that, with the electric scooter, with a prosthetic like my superbike, I would devour the world. It wouldn't just bring me from school to the dorm and from the dorm to the school, it would also take me down unimaginable paths to places I had never even dreamed of, with colors I had never seen.

I've gone to NASA. I was granted a Guinness World Record (handed to me by the best speaker in the world, Josep Trabal) for being the first person to build a functioning prosthetic arm with LEGO pieces. I've been to Hong Kong. I've visited LEGO headquarters and learned to expand my project with the best people in LEGO Education. I was born without an arm, and my family held me. They gave me strength, offered me all their love. I fell and picked myself up. I put together LEGOs with just one hand. My bike became too small, and my father built me a prosthetic. I fell and just lay there, but then I got up. I faced my fears and my bullies. We built another prosthetic for the bike. I fell and didn't get back up; my heart was broken. I came back stronger after repeating a year. I built the MK-1. Then the MK-2. I elaborated various prosthetics during the LEGO Education program. At just twenty years old, a documentary was made about my life. And now, a few projects later, I'm at the MK-5.

But nothing, absolutely nothing, would have been possible without the support of my family, my father's persistence (which I inherited), my mother's and sister's affection, my friends' pride, the perseverance and stubbornness I've always been known for, and the eternal love of my grand-parents Joan and Basilisa, who have always been with me, ever since Abu Basi wrapped me in her white swaddling cloth.

Before saying goodbye, I want you to stop reading and once more count your fingers.

One,

two,

three,

four . . .

Well, I think you can stop here, because however many there are, you'll never lack any of them if you know you're whole.

ACKNOWLEDGMENTS

"If life takes something away from you, look around you.

The piece that will put you back together is at your fingertips."

—David Aguilar

Basilisa Cordero Patrocinio «àvia Basi» (*Sempre al nostre cor*)

Joan Aguilar Clà

Gilbert Amphoux «Avi» (*Toujours dans notre cœur*)

Josette Balada «Tati Jojo»

Joan Aguilar Ornosa

Nathalie Amphoux «Mamá»

Naia Aguilar Amphoux «Sister»

Diana Aguilar Cordero

Xavier Aguilar Ornosa

Joan Carles Aguilar Cordero

Amandine Amphoux

Romain Amphoux

Frédéric Amphoux «Tonton»

Lina Herrero Talavera «àvia
Lina»

Ferran Jerez Herrero «tiet
Fernan»

Emma Jerez

Teo Jerez

Carolina d'Areny Plandolit

Meritxell Álvarez Plata
d'Areny Plandolit

Javier Hernández Alejandrino

Rosa Moya

Manoli Hernández
Alejandrino

Imc Agencia Literaria

Isabel Martí Castro

Eva Pinel

Jordi Ribolleda (Ribu)

Jordi Carbonell

Penguin Random House

Laia Zamarrón

Berta Martín

Anna Jolis

Arlong Productions

David Ortiz Simón

Juanjo Ojeda

Egrafics

Enrique Muñoz

Doodle Carbon

Sergi Bardia

Lluís Valls

E.Leclerc Punt de Trobada

Jordi Cachafeiro

Jordi Cachafeiro Jr.

**Fan N.1 de David en el
Líbano**

Karim Kabani & Family

Jordi De Miguel—Demi

Enic Torres Cortina

Robert Marsal

Vallnord

Jennifer Ferrer

Josep Marticella

Pedro Morán

Bomosa

Turi Mora

Manel Garcia

X-Pirience la Seu d'Urgell

Joan Erola

Marc Vicente

Eva Gispert

Joan Vilella

Silvia Pantebre

Manolo Contreras García

Manel Contreras Pérez

Montse Pérez Ortiz

Claudia Contreras Pérez

Viatges Emocions

Mari Carmen Jorquera

Microfusa

Adrian Federigi

LEGO Group

Thanks to each and every one of the employees and managers of LEGO for the support and admiration you have demonstrated over the history of my *superación*. Thanks for working so hard and making possible the dreams of all the children of the world and helping them to develop their creativity to build a better world.

Niels B. Christiansen
    (CEO LEGO Group)

Troy Taylor

César Ridruejo

Britt Denise Lauritsen

Tormod Askildsen

Kiki Chan

Yannick Dupont

Houda Abbes

Alina Cojocaru

Claudette Muñoz

Esben Staerk

Nina Koesman

Vivi K.schalagelverger

Isabel Perez Sanchez

Helene Giroux

LEGO Education

LEGO Group

LEGO House

Edacom México

Carlos Enríquez Pérez
    González «Willys I»

Erika Valenzuela Alarcón
   «Willys 2»
Karla Rebeca Pérez Valenzuela
   «Willys 3»
Ana Paola Pérez Valenzuela
   «Willys 4»
María Fernanda Martínez

Sonnos Andorra
Pere Revert
Miguel Espinosa
Carlos Lozano

El Programa De AR
Julio López Uzal

LinkedIn
Jennifer Bonilla
Aurore Vuadelle

Inokim Spain
Quim Cassany
Xavier Raventós
Joan Maria
Cassany
Marc Cassany
Kfir Benshooshan
Yoshi Bluth

Hebo
Jonathan Lozano

Maker Faire Galicia
Marcos Saavedra
Enrique Saavedra

Grifone
Lluis Albert Morera

MoraBanc
Francesc Mora
Lluís Alsina
Pedro González
Miguel Antonio Pérez
Mireia Maestre
Josep Lluís Trabal
Yolanda Banqueri
Xavier Riestra
Carlos Salinas
Cristina Vilanova
Ferran Vila
Sanae Lamrani
Josep Maria Rodríguez
Enric Fernández
Sergi Montané
Ignasi Lasheras
Sonia Torres

Carles Valen

Isabel Gimenez

Tal3ntia

Saúl Larrayad Porroche

MRC

Francesc Aroca

Manel Reyes

Moraband Members

Mireia Maestre

Ramón Aranda

Lluís Molina

Bernat Decatalogne

Carlos Salinas

Xavier Riestra

Eduardo Cunha

Josep Anton Flecha

Tomás García Purriños

Josep Maria Rodríguez

Carles Figueras

Miriam Navarrete

Sergi García

Patricia Medina

Rosa Pastor

Retrobant

David Pérez Saavedra

Chus Saavedra

Ferran Pérez Lenza

Carlos Almeida

Amador González

Sebastián López Rodríguez

Antoni Flores Cano

Teodoro Martínez Rubio

Asunción López

Biel Núñez Martínez

Airana Núñez Martínez

Ana Martínez López

Javier Martínez López

Lluis Gonzàlez

**To all the parents, students
and teachers of Escola
Auró Barcelona**

Maribel Espinosa

Manuel Marín

Víctor Marín Espinosa (*Pronto*
Magazine)

Joan Carles Sasplugas
Montse Mateu
Josep Gironell i Roig
Xavier Bielsa Palacín
Manel Gironell i Bielsa

Idneo "Dreammaker Team"
Josep Maria Pujol
Montse Ibáñez
Raúl Lucas
Artur Opi

English Summer Tamarit

Col·legi Sant Ermengol
Carmen
Berta
Anna
Alex
Ramon
Carmina
Maria Josep
Naiara
Brine
Lina
Rosa Mari
Pepi
Xavi

Muller
Carmen
Itziar
Josefina
Lluis Gras
Joan

National Geographic España—RBA Revistas
Pep Cabello Guilera
Pau Fabregat Adell
Teresa Esmatges Dedéu
Eva van den Berg

Augé Grup
Jordi Auge Sánchez
Pere Auge Sánchez

UNICEF Andorra
Marta Alberch

Naturland
Hble. Comú de Sant Julià de Lòria

Raquel López Montes
Juan Pablo González Solís
Rubén González López

Paula González López

Jordi Checa

Ruth Ponce

AFANIP

Autea

FAAD—Federació Andorrana
   d'Associacions de Persones
   amb Discapacitat

Amida

AAMA

Amare

AMPA-EENSM

Trana

Anselmo Callejo Ferreras y
   Familia

Carlos Sánchez Valverde y
   Familia

Lluís Barba Gómez y Familia

Lidie Paoli

Stéphane Philippe

Yamina Doumi

Daniel Philippe

Neus Majoral Mill

Pere Matamales

Jordi Matamales Majoral

Aleix Matamales Majoral

Pilar Calvo

Darwish Kurdi

Viva-Technology

Stéphane Barbot

Ernesto Martínez-Villalpando

Álex García Sánchez

Pau Bascompte

Cristina Bascompte

Maria Arques Rubio

LaminAnd

Olga Moran

Oriol Ruiz

Oriol Murcia

Joan Mesalles

David Oriol

Josep Arasanz

Judit Pintat

Maria Quimeso

Marc Boixader

Ingrid Bertran

Joan Albós

Ariadna Villalta

Carla Vela

Sergi Balmes

Yuri Quella

Joan Llobet

Ainoa Angrill

Eric Tarragó

Ingrid Bertran

Mario Agudo

Tomás Agudo

Ainoa Angrill

Adrian Jauregui

Carolina Martos

Erik Calvente

Irene Gómez

Helena Jori

Gema Planella

Véronique Malique

Mossèn Xavier Pares Saltor

Annie Muracciole «Touillette»

Joaquim Gil

Unihabit Sant Cugat

Montse Orozco

Dennis Fuentes Zabala

Éric Fuentes Zavala

Evelyn Vera Bejar

UIC-Universitat Internacional de Catalunya

Yusara Kispe

Jaume Figa Vaello

Roman Pérez

To all my class companies and teachers of UIC Bioengineering UIC-Universitat Internacional de Catalunya in Sant Cugat, Barcelona.

XXVII Cumbre Iberoamericana—Andorra 2020

To all the ministers of social affairs of the 27th Cumbre Iberoamericana in Andorra, 2020.

To its president Rebeca Grynspan Mayufis, Protocol Department of the Govern d'Andorra.

Coprincep d'Andorra i Bisbe d'Urgell

Joan-Enric Vives i Sicília

To all the leaders and institutions of my country.

Govern d'Andorra
Xavier Espot Zamora
Ester Fenoll García
Jordi Gallardo Fernández
Victor Filloy Franco
Joan Martínez Benazet
Ester Vilarrubla Escales
Silvia Riva González
Judit Pallares Cortes
Jordi Torres Falcó
Silvia Calvó Armengol
Verònica Canals Riba
Eric Jover Comas
Maria Ubach Font
Josep Maria Rossell Pons

Actua
Marc Pons
Carme López

Gilbert Saboya Sunyé
Josep Maria Missé Cortina

To the entire population of Andorra for their love and affection.

Andorra Sostenible

Bàsquet Club Andorra
Gabriel Fernández Coy
Gorka Aixas

Former Health Minister of Spain
María Luisa Carcedo Roces

Dir. Comunicación Ministerio de Sanidad
Miriam Lorenzo Fernández

Yannick Dupont
Leo Duppont
Aurelien Rouffiange
Lee Magpili
Markus Crossman

RightThisMinute TV
Oli Pettigrew
Gayle Bass
Nick Calderone
Charity Bailey
Madi Lipari
Christian Vera

Deluxe
Jorge Javier Vázquez

Hora Punta
Javier Cárdenas
Alejandra Castelló
Jokin Buesa

CNN—Great Big Story
Connor Boals
Austin Brown

Tvemos Informatius TV3

Informativos RTVE

Informativos Tele 5

Cocina Abierta
Karlos Arguiñano

Guinness World Records
Craig Glenday

Ligue Universelle du Bien Public
Nicole Crignon (Veuve Bernard Ricard)

Jean Claude Baudry

Embajada de Andorra en París
Cristina Rodríguez Galán

TF1
Thierry Coiffier
Sébastien Maloiseaux
Karina Dabrowski

Chester on Cuatro
Risto Mejide
Christian Gálvez

Lleida TV
Marivi Chacon

Brut
Kombini

Para Todos La2
Dolors Elias

Volverte a ver
Carlos Sobera

La que se avecina
Pablo Chiapella

Revista Dona Secret
Josep Segura
Nelly Dedea

Diari d'Andorra
El Periòdic d'Andorra
RTVA
BonDia
ARA Andorra
ANA (Agència de Notícies d'Andorra)

La Vanguardia—La Contra
Ima Sanchís

Les Echos
Benoît Georges

Vodafone. El futuro es apasionante
Noelia Nùñez

ANA—Agència de Notícies d'Andorra Foto Clic
Sonu Tublani
Carlos Almeida

Big Karma
Pascal Clarysse

Let's Go Festival Brasil— Positivo Tecnología
Luis Augusto Matiello
Leandro Freitas
Álvaro Luis Cruz

NASA Cross Industry Innovation Summit 2019

NASA—National Aeronautics and Space Administration
Nikki Eberhardt
Dimitris Bountolos (currently Chief Information & Innovation Officer at Ferrovial)
Omar Atamleh
Ramon Vullings
Charlie Wen (Marvel Studios cofounder)
Frank Stephenson

Hotel Lautrec Opéra-París
Mr. Elie Marcos et famille

Foto Estudi la Seu
José Sánchez
Anna Moliné

Mari Carmen Jorquera

Ernesto Martínez Villalpando

Casa Vicens

Mercedes Mora

Emili Masferrer

TV3 Catalunya

Rosa Talamás

Lluís Marquina

Toni Cruanyes

Imminent Produccions

José Pozo

Elisabet Terry

Ascensors Sales

Francesc Sales

Alex Molina

Anna Villas—Escola Sant

Ermengol

La Vanguardia

Rosa Matas

Peggy Cerqueda

Dra. Mari Carmen Doncel

Dr. Jesús Benito

Nostra Senyora de Meritxell Hospital

Josep Maria Piqué

Dr. Carranza

Albert Batalla

Serralleria Pirineus

Jordi

Joan

Embajada de España en Andorra

Ángel Ros

Enrique Conde

Nicolás del Busto

Xavier Sanjurjo

Storytelling Comunicació

Toni Corominas

Confederació d'Empresaris d'Andorra (CEA)

Gerard Cadena

Fundación Adecco

Alicia Oliva

Pablo García

Héctor Clemente

Marta Martín

Keitas Systems
Lahou Keita

**OBAP—Organization
of Black Aerospace
Professionals**
Jean Olivier Mbog

**WBAF—World Business
Angels Investment Forum**
Baybars Altuntas

Airbus
Natalia Muñoz
José María Palomino
Moises Guitierrez

Museo Thyssen
Guillermo Cervera
Marta Codinach
Charline Bony
Teresa Areny

Purpose Alliance
Francisco Palao

Brand Solo
Jordi Verdura

**International School
Education**
BEST-Bilingual Education
Summit
María Eugenia Bittencourt
Ulisses Cardinot

BYUp Ecuador
Ana Barrera
Diana de la Torre
Hernán Schuster

Medtronic
Paulo Carvalho

Futurum Careers
Karen Lindsay

La Sexta-Zapeando
Dani Mateo
Maya Pxelskaya

Studio 10 (Australia)
Celestina Ramljak
Sarah Harrys
Tristan Mac

Fernando Domínguez
(México)

P.I. Advocats

Ester Peralba García

Miguel Ángel Rodríguez

Margarita Bértolo

Arun Bahirwani

Fundació Jacqueline Pradère

Pyrénées Andorra

Patrick Pérez Pradere

Cristina Urbiola de Pérez

Iván Armengod

Josep Manzano
  Castellblanqué

Evelyne Breut

Maria Teresa Casas

The Walt Disney Company

Dibujante de cómics

Víctor Félix-Díaz

Matti Hammi

Holger Paasch

**BSA—BancSabadell
  d'Andorra**

Josep Segura

Mireia Montoriol

Miquel Alavern

Albert Llovera Massana

Marcel Llovera Massana

Núria Coll Llovera

Carmen Monviedro

Xavier Llovera

**RTVA—Radio i Televisió
  d'Andorra**

Rosa Alberch

Xavi Mujal

Meritxell Bellosta

González-Bueno SLP

Pablo González Bueno

Caldea

Miguel Pedregal

Surf Evasió

Gilles Bony et famille

Grup Gong—La Adelita

Juan Carlos Valladares Riestra

Filmax International

Carlos Fernández

Laura Fernández

Iván Díaz

Carlos Rojano

Jaime Otto López Carballeda

Miranda López

Chelo Esteban

Anna Parramon

Carmen Rivera

Juan Carlos Orellana Torres

Sandra Benamor

Anna Majoral

Joan Ramon Peña

Ingrid López

**Friends forever (ex-colleagues
from Barclays Bank)**

**Barclays (Territorial
Catalunya)**

Amaya Cordon

Cecilia Moreno, «Ceci»

Domingo Luna

Fernando Dominguez

Joan Carles Pinto

Jordi Buxons

Jordi Enseñat

Jordi Espelt

María Esther Rubio

Miriam Castillejo

Nuria Zambrano

Pepe Arruga

Salvador Juárez

Jenaro Millet Capella

Sebastián López

Miriam Salazar

Fran Arrebola

Lourdes Gorriz

Maria Lamas

Xavier Mayor

**Ludoescola de Sant Julià
de Lòria**

Ferreteria Llevet

Josep Llevet

Teresa Llevet

Fundació Jacqueline Pradere

Seeds of Respect

Alvaro Prades

Esteve Baques

Edgar Brull

Ignacio Capella

Inés Suris

Oracle

Guillermo Ruiz Esteban

Kars Andorra

Joan Sala

Carmén Sala

Joan Gómez

Daniel Gómez Sala

LEGO MASTERS
  FRANCE S1
Endemol Shine France
M6

Sebastien et David

Eric Antoine

George Schmitt

Paulina Aubey

Loic et Guillaume

Maximilien et Thibault

Christelle et Johan

Ariana et Aurélien

Xavier et Alban

Marguerite et Renaud

Yann et Jean-Phillippe

Vladimir Slimitch

Fiona Bochatay

Julien Randria

Julien Aubourg

LEGO MASTERS
  ESPAÑA S1

Stephan y Victor

Roberto Leal

Eva Hache

Pablo Gonzalez

Begoña y Pedro

Javier y Alfonso

Claudia y Ana

Sandra y Jero

Nati y Miguel

Marina y Miguel

Daniel y Ángeles

ANDORRA 2027
FIS ALPINE WORLD
SKI CHAMPIONSHIPS
SOLDEU-EL TARTER
OF GRANDVALIRA
CANDIDATE

Elisabeth Perez

David Hidalgo

Irene Gómez

Rosa Rubio

RocaJunyent
Joaquim Matinero Tor

Illa Carlemany
Cinemes Illa Carlemany
Automòbil Club d'Andorra
Circuit del Pas de la Casa
Restaurant L'Ovella Negra

Kine
Jordi Obiols

Becier
Pere Betriu
David Majoral

Hand Solo NFTs Voice Note
Amrita Sethi
Anil Sethi

Nexxyo Labs (Outer Ring video game)
Daniel Valdes
Ricardo Cevallos
Pedro Miranda
Ignacio Ferrer
Jose Luis Sanjurjo
Nekane Esquinas
María Alejandra Figueroa

Beknur's Family
Beknur Zhanibekuly
Nur Sultan
Zaure Bektemissova
Janibek Bektemisov

SHINE IBERIA
Macarena Rey

Tina Baldeon
Lina Gomez
Ana Palmeiro
Raúl Grijalvo

Jesus Mazo Ber

Ayúdame 3D
Guillermo Martinez Gauna
    Vivas

SEAT
Laura Vidal Tost
Alberto Daniel Fernandez
    Garcia
Felix Diaz Sanchez
Wayne Griffiths
Ursula Wiedemann
Dr. Werner J. Tietz
Antonino Labate
Jordi Torrente
Teresa Forradelles
Oriol Mas
Sara Martin Benitez

VISTA DIFERENT
Miquel Liso Guitart
Xavier Liso Guitart
Cristina Prat

PIENSO, LUEGO ACTÚO.
(YOIGO social media
platform)
Pepo Jimenez
Zaira Gordo
Javier Garrido
Alberto Gonzalez
Ivan Arruza
Facundo Andrés

HAND SOLO (BRAND)
Pere Matamales
Alex Dotti

**MICHEL LAFON
PUBLISHING SA**
Elsa Lafon
Margaux Russo

**Beijing Yuchen Culture Co.
Ltd**
Yao Xiangzliu

Psichogios Publications S.A.
Nikolaos Psichogios

Agora S.A.

**Asset and Capital Advisers,
SL**
Jesus Hidalgo Quesada
José Miguel Barrera Borruel
(Chemi)

Scenic Rights
Sydney Borjas Piloto

AMAZON
Mouncif Faqir

TRALDIS PORTA S.L.
Jordi Porta Barral
Agustí Porta Barral
Jordi Porta Miró
Carles Porta Miró
Ruben Eduardo Muñoz
Yolanda Riubrugent
Javier Cabello
Jaume Pla
Vicenç Reche
Josep Rubio
Josep Maria Clauso
*And the rest of the team with
love*

Moonshot Pirates

Lenka Bacova

Tero Moliis

Edelman

Debbie Fagan

James Woods

Remy Guasch

Alison Harmon

Gerard Estrada

Laurence Favrel

Thais Estrada

Ingrid Estrada

David Lectures

IDAPA Mobile Week La Seu d'Urgell

Agora International School Andorra

Ajuntament de la Seu d'Urgell

SwissQ Consulting AG— Swiss Testing Day

Ecorys UK Ltd.

Ministerio de Educación— Municipio de Leon, Guanajuato (México)

Shackleton SL for Atento

Companies collaborating with the Adecco Foundation in Spain to promote the inclusion of people with disabilities, including:

ALTEN

Talgo

Airbus

Ultracongelados Virto

JD Sports

Pepsico

Cafte

Sdg

Barna Steel

Zucchetti

Free Now

OHL

Thanks

We only live once to be thankful.

Dedicated to all those who have collaborated
in David's personal growth.

ABOUT THE AUTHORS

Photo © José Sánchez, Foto Estudi La Seu

David Aguilar and his father, Ferran Aguilar, are from Andorra, in Europe. David was born missing part of one arm. At the age of nine, he designed his first prosthesis with LEGO bricks, and in high school he built the next generation, which he named the MK-1. His father encouraged him to make a video about his prosthesis and the huge role that LEGOs played in his life, and posted it on social media, where it went viral and changed both of their lives. In addition to telling his story in a book, David is also the protagonist of the Spanish documentary *Mr. Hand Solo*, which won the award for best documentary at the Boston Science Fiction Film festival. David is currently developing his own brand, Hand Solo, which will aim to benefit various organizations for the disabled and fight against the stigma of "diff-ability," as he calls it.

Connect with David and Ferran online:
Twitter David: @Handsolooficial
Twitter Ferran: @AguilarFerran

Instagram David: @handsoloofficial
Instagram Ferran: @nanoseu

Facebook David: Hand Solo
Facebook Ferran: Ferran Aguilar Cordero

LinkedIn David: David Aguilar aka Hand Solo
LinkedIn Ferran: Ferran Aguilar

www.handsolo.com

ABOUT THE TRANSLATOR

Photo © 2021 Lawrence Schimel

Lawrence Schimel is a bilingual author who writes in both Spanish and English, with more than one hundred books to his credit. He is also a prolific literary translator, into English and into Spanish. His translated books include Wanda Gág's *Millions of Cats*; George Takei's graphic novel

They Called Us Enemy; and *Some Days*, written and illustrated by María Wernicke; among many others. He lives in Madrid, Spain. Follow him on Twitter @lawrenceschimel.